ROUTLEDGE LIBRARY EDITIONS:
AUTOBIOGRAPHY

Volume 4

V.S. NAIPAUL:
DISPLACEMENT AND AUTOBIOGRAPHY

V.S. NAIPAUL: DISPLACEMENT AND AUTOBIOGRAPHY

JUDITH LEVY

Routledge
Taylor & Francis Group
LONDON AND NEW YORK

First published in 1995

This edition first published in 2016
by Routledge
2 Park Square, Milton Park, Abingdon, Oxon OX14 4RN

and by Routledge
711 Third Avenue, New York, NY 10017

Routledge is an imprint of the Taylor & Francis Group, an informa business

British Library Cataloguing in Publication Data
A catalogue record for this book is available from the British Library

ISBN: 978-1-138-93641-6 (Set)
ISBN: 978-1-315-67463-6 (Set) (ebk)
ISBN: 978-1-138-93937-0 (Volume 4) (hbk)
ISBN: 978-1-138-94204-2 (Volume 4) (pbk)
ISBN: 978-1-315-67461-2 (Volume 4) (ebk)

Publisher's Note
The publisher has gone to great lengths to ensure the quality of this reprint but points out that some imperfections in the original copies may be apparent.

Disclaimer
The publisher has made every effort to trace copyright holders and would welcome correspondence from those they have been unable to trace.

V. S. NAIPAUL

Displacement and Autobiography

Judith Levy

GARLAND PUBLISHING, INC.
New York & London / 1995

Library of Congress Cataloging-in-Publication Data

Levy, Judith, 1945–
V. S. Naipaul : displacement and autobiography / Judith Levy.
p. cm. — (Garland reference library of the humanities ; v. 1781)
Includes bibliographical references and index.
ISBN 0-8153-1468-X (alk. paper)
1. Naipaul, V. S. (Vidiadhar Surajprasad), 1932– —Criticism and interpretation. 2. Alienation (Social psychology) in literature. 3. Cultural relations in literature. 4. Culture conflict in literature. 5. West Indies—In literature. 6. Self in literature. 7. Autobiography. I. Title. II. Series.
PR9272.9.N32Z758 1995
823'.914—dc20 94-37551
CIP

Printed on acid-free, 250-year-life paper
Manufactured in the United States of America

To my parents

Contents

Acknowledgments

This book could not have been written without the continued support and invaluable critique of Shlomith Rimmon-Kenan who has been both a mentor and a friend. It has also benefited immeasurably by the reading and comments of H. M. Dalesky, to whom I am very grateful. I would, in addition, like to thank John Landau and Daphne Leighton for their unflagging interest and for the stimulating discussions we have had over the years.

The Hebrew University, Jerusalem, the University of Wisconsin at Madison and the Lady Davis Foundation made it possible for me to spend a year, 1991-92, at the University of Wisconsin working on the final version of the book. There, Todd Bender provided a much-needed anchor of encouragement and counsel. I am also grateful to Ms Adelle Perlov for undertaking to copyedit and proofread the final manuscript.

I would like to thank Aitken, Stone & Wylie Limited for permission to quote copyright material from the works of V. S. Naipaul.

Introduction

V. S. Naipaul, a Trinidadian of Indian descent living in the West, mainly in England, has written in many forms: the short story, the novella, the novel, the travel book, the essay, the history, the autobiographical account, and the book review. Through an analysis of five works by Naipaul written in different modes and periods of his life, this study posits a relationship between a cultural condition and a choice of genre, or more specifically, between cultural displacement and the writing of autobiography. It thus examines an aspect of Naipaul's development as a post-colonial writer, and, by extension, explores the way concepts of self determine the writing of texts.

The basic proposition underlying my reading and informing my entire undertaking is that a fundamental impetus of Naipaul's writing is to create a self,[1] which, in textual terms, is to write autobiography; that the writing of an autobiography is for Naipaul conditional on the acquisition of a myth of origin; and that this condition is thwarted by a split that constitutes his cultural dislocation. I am further proposing that the undermining of the autobiographical purpose results in works that I have chosen to call deflected autobiographies, which may shed some light on the destabilizing of genre boundaries and definitions in current thinking. Finally, through the chronological spacing of the works I have selected, I trace what I see in Naipaul's writing life as a two-fold, interdependent process: from the enactment of the split and the severance from the colonial past, through different stages in the quest for origin and for a form in which to find and express self, to resolution—the creation of a myth of origin and the construction of a post-colonial self through the writing of an autobiography.[2]

Naipaul's writing life, as I see it, has been constituted by a cultural split for which the Lacanian concept of the accession into the symbolic order and concomitant processes can be seen as both paradigm and metaphor.[3] In the Lacanian constellation, the accession into language, which is also the resolution of the Oedipus complex, acts as a means to ground the subject in reality, while the repressed pre-verbal world[4] comes to constitute the void, the lost part of oneself, the lack which is, however, repeatedly reenacted symbolically through the signifying chain. However, the resolution of the Oedipal complex which accompanies the accession into the symbolic order also involves the compensation for the repressed desire for the mother through the identification with the father, or through the accession to the Name-of-the-Father and his Law. Thus, the relinquishing of the primal tie with the mother augurs the gain of social structure, civilization and, hence, history. In the creation of a subject, then, the repressed, the longing for undifferentiated wholeness, or origin, is replaced by a collectively conceived and perpetuated past, or what I have chosen to call a myth of origin.

My use of the term myth of origin is intentional and includes the contradictory usage to which the concept of myth has been put: a creation, a story of origin in the traditional sense, and, conversely, an illusion of origin in Derridean Deconstruction. Myth, according to the dictionary, is "a usually traditional story of ostensibly historical events that serves to unfold part of the world view of a people or explain a practice, belief, or natural phenomenon" (*Webster's New Collegiate Dictionary*, 1988). In that sense, the myth of origin that in my concept is a crucial condition for the emergence of self is a received story, in cultural terms the heritage that comes with the Law of the Father. At the same time, equally fundamental in my formulation is the Deconstructionist notion of origin or centre as an illusory construct, a substitute (and I am consciously avoiding the problem of whether what the myth comes to replace is merely irrevocably lost or never existed): "Henceforth, it became necessary to think both the law which somehow governed the desire for a center . . . and the process of signification which orders the displacements and substitutions for this law of central presence—but a central presence which has never been itself, has always already been exiled from itself into its own substitute. The substitute does not substitute itself for anything which has somehow existed before it."[5] Derrida replaces origin with discourse: "This was the moment when language invaded the universal problematic, the moment when, in the absence of a center or origin, everything became discourse—provided we can agree on this word—that is to say, a system in which the central signified, the original or transcendental signified, is never absolutely present outside a system of differences."[6] The relationship of discourse to origin in Derrida has affinities with Lacan's concept of the subject constituted in the symbolic order. This is a subject who comes into being only through lack of origin and with the insertion into language.

This individual developmental process can, as I have said, serve as a metaphor for a cultural situation shared by Naipaul and other writers brought up under colonial rule and struggling to find a place in a post-colonial world. The decision to become a writer in the English language and tradition was taken by Naipaul in childhood. However, by accepting the language and education of the colonizing British Empire, he was taking on a usurper Father with his own Law. It was not only the pre-verbal world of the mother, i.e., "origin," that had to be repressed and denied in order to accede into language, but the Name of the Father associated with the "real" Father too, his law, his language and history. The repudiation of the past is thus not only that of the primal mother, but of a whole culture, in this case the Indian-Hindu heritage in its Trinidadian metamorphosis, the history that should have constituted the myth of origin. Thus, the accession into the alien symbolic order and language inevitably involves a severance from origin both personal *and* collective. The acquired usurping language cannot instill a past in the subject, and the past is barred from constituting a sense of self.[7]

It is necessary at this point to define my use of the term "self," which touches on my work in two ways: one, as a component—*autos*—of writing autobiography, which will be dealt with further on in this introduction; and two, as an ontological concept. It is beyond the scope and purpose of this study to enter into the polemics of the ontological status of "self." The classical, Cartesian-based "self," which, as Janet Gunn points out, is "not only private and hidden . . . it is also timeless and unchanging . . ."[8] has been seriously undermined by the scrutiny of postmodernist thinking. In its extreme form this probing of the concept in relation to the world, to time, and—in autobiography—to writing, has led to the pronouncement of the "death" of the writing self by such authors as Foucault, De Man, Barthes and others,[9] who, by asserting the primacy of writing, have in various ways declared self to be nothing more than a linguistic construct. Such conclusions, the inexorable logic of which seems at times inescapable, are not useful for the purposes of this undertaking which is interested precisely in the relationship of the constructions of self to the production of text. I wish to combine the acknowledgment of the split subject and the absence that determines the nature of our existence in the world with the subjective self (its ontological status whatever it may be) that is at the basis of our *experience* of the world. I have preferred not to limit my use of the term "self" to Lacan's Imaginary, where it might seem to belong, precisely because I am interested in that entity, which Lacan strives to undo, in which the Imaginary and the Symbolic co-exist, fuse or disrupt one another. In other words, my analysis, while employing what might be called externally imposed diagnostic tools, makes room for the internal experience, deceptive as it may be. Thus in this study, to have a sense of self is conditional on being a subject with a myth of origin, and all the instances in which the word "self" appears presuppose that connection.

It is important to point out that I am utilizing the Lacanian paradigm as a metaphor for Naipaul's cultural predicament and not as a means to understand his personal biography, although the two do, of course, overlap. In his works, the act of writing, i.e., life in the symbolic order, is often seen to be equivalent to living or creating a sense of self: "So while, when I travel, I can move only according to what I find, I also live, as it were, in a novel of my own making, moving from not knowing to knowing, with person interweaving with person and incident opening out into incident."[10] Naipaul's life, then, necessarily comes into this study insofar as it is the subject of the split between the symbolic order and the pre-verbal world as it appears in his writings.

At the risk of schematization and reductiveness, I have divided Naipaul's writings into three phases: an early phase of fiction writing, from his arrival in London in 1954, following his studies at Oxford, until about 1961–62, from which I have chosen to discuss *A House for Mr Biswas* (1960); a middle phase of two decades or so of extensive travel during which his writing is split almost equally between fiction and non-fiction (travel books, histories and journalism), from which I will discuss *The Overcrowded Barracoon* (1972) and *In a Free State* (1971); and a third phase, from about 1982, which I would like to call the phase of resolution, during which, alongside additional fiction and travel books, Naipaul has produced what I define as his autobiography. From this phase I shall discuss two works: *Finding the Centre* (1984) and *The Enigma of Arrival* (1987).

The decision taken by Naipaul in childhood to become a writer involved more than finding a place for the self to inhabit after having rejected the claustrophobic squalor of his family life in Trinidad. The voyage to England symbolically represented the conscious embracing of the English language and culture as a substitute heritage and the repudiation of the past which was felt as a vacuum: ". . . but it was really an expression of dissatisfaction at the emptiness of our own formless, unmade society. To us, without a mythology, all literatures were foreign."[11] But writing, as the means of creating a self, in itself produced formidable dilemmas, not the least being problems arising from the choice of materials and form, and the status of the past in the present. As Naipaul himself has stated at various points in his life,[12] the reality of being an outsider in England, in contrast to the nurtured fantasy of England, forced him to turn to the past for his materials, even while denying its validity as a myth of origin. At the same time, the form he used was that of the English novel for which he knew no alternative. The only examples of "Trinidadian" literature which had served him as a model were short stories written by his father, Seepersad Naipaul.[13] Finally, unable to embark on the creation of self without some concept of origin, Naipaul began his writing career by inventing for himself what I would call a myth of non-origin,[14] thus reconciling the contradiction of standing by his denial of the past with the establishing of a self.

From this phase, the attempt to mould himself into the "English" writer of novels using Trinidadian materials, I shall discuss *A House for Mr Biswas*, the culminating work of the early period. Written in the tradition of nineteenth-century English fiction, it enacts the problem of the split and its concomitant severance from origin, and is at the same time a deflected autobiographical novel. As a fictional biography of Naipaul's father, it dramatizes the loss of a myth of origin both through his father's life (the structure of which is repeated in his own life) and in the relationship between his father and himself delineated in the novel.

The second phase of Naipaul's career begins, in my division, following the writing of *A House for Mr Biswas* (and subsequently of *Mr Stone and the Knights Companion* [1963]), which brought the problem of the relationship of self and the past to the fore (albeit implicitly). This was coupled with a dual disillusionment: with himself in the role of English novelist, and with fiction as a vehicle for the creation and expression of self.[15] This phase is marked by a giving up of what was now seen as a false base and an embarkation on a sublimated quest for origin and form. His extensive travelling at this time, for example, enacts both the correlation between living and writing, i.e., life in the symbolic order as the only means to create self, what Peter Hughes has called "travelling to write,"[16] and the condition of no-place, i.e., no origin. In his writing the quest takes two forms: an intellectual exploration of the causes and effects of colonialism, of the Third World, and the concept of history, and the experimentation with non-fictional modes such as the travel book, history writing, and journalism alongside the continued writing of fiction.

The two works I have chosen to discuss from this period are *The Overcrowded Barracoon*, a collection of essays, and *In a Free State*, a work of fiction. Each embodies an aspect of the relation of Naipaul's quest for origin, self and literary form at this time. The first, *The Overcrowded Barracoon*, presents an interesting example for the analysis of contemporary autobiography theorists' attempt to redefine autobiography while delegitimizing existing genre definitions. On the one hand, it records a period in Naipaul's life of a surface absenting of self and the projection, through travel, of personal concerns onto societies, history and other intellectual issues. On the other, in its underlying themes and through the retrospective ordering and organizing of the material, it can be seen as an autobiographical act.[17] Thus, in addition to its interest as representing an important phase in Naipaul's oeuvre, *The Overcrowded Barracoon* is briefly discussed in terms of its problematization of current thinking on autobiography.

The second work, *In a Free State,* also has travelling as a major theme, and like the other fictional works of this phase, thematizes the condition of "no self" through characters who are continually split between an insufficient present and a lost past. *In a Free State*, however, also evinces the beginning of Naipaul's manipulation of the fictional and the non-fictional to create a truer expression of self.

The third phase of Naipaul's works, is, as I have said, a phase of resolution. Here I am delineating two major steps: the first, a confrontation, a consequence of the subtle "working through" of the previous phase, with his lack of a myth of origin, not, as in the early years, through denial, but through recognition and acceptance; and the second, the creation of self and, by extension, the writing of autobiography, made possible by the creation of a myth of origin.

Finding the Centre (1984) is composed of two narratives: "Prologue to an Autobiography," the closest declared intention on Naipaul's part to write an autobiography, and "The Crocodiles of Yamoussoukro," an account of a trip to the Ivory Coast. In "Prologue to an Autobiography" the source of the ambition to become a writer and the concomitant void created in the self are traced and acknowledged. In "The Crocodiles of Yamoussoukro" the relation of origin to myth and reality is examined through a travel experience in Africa which becomes symbolic. *Finding the Centre*, in other words, reinforces through its structure Naipaul's split between writing and history, the symbolic order and origin. At the same time, by bringing these two narratives together in one book Naipaul not only creates links between them that obscure the boundaries between history and fiction, but also seems to suggest the possible future creation of an autobiographical narrative through conscious mythologizing.

The Enigma of Arrival, the last book to be discussed, is, as I see it, Naipaul's autobiography: the product of the construction of a myth of origin, i.e., of a post-colonial self, and the finding of the appropriate mode, a merging of history and fiction, in which to write it. Interestingly, while much postmodern writing has obscured the boundaries between autobiography and the novel by having the author insert himself/herself into the fiction as a character, in *The Enigma of Arrival* the opposite is true. All the facts are biographically verifiable, but it is the mode which is novelistic. *The Enigma of Arrival* is a painstaking account of being "reborn" into the English landscape in middle age. Through a myth of "arrival" it weaves cycles of life and death and locates the writer's previous life in relation to the birth of this new identity. By manipulating the autobiographical and novelistic mode Naipaul uses postmodern devices to create a genre which becomes a reflection of his theme.[18]

My discussion of Naipaul's works in the following chapters, then, traces the problems of self as reflected in his work thematically, structurally and in relation to the writing of autobiography. It does not pretend to be an exhaustive study or monograph on V. S. Naipaul as writer. Not only are certain preoccupations and foci of his writings, especially political, left out, but only five out of a corpus of almost twenty books, not including his numerous essays, articles and book reviews, are considered in depth. Naipaul's controversial political stand and the animosity it has generated,[19] have only been referred to if and when they shed light on my main objective, which is to examine the underlying split and dislocation that inform Naipaul's works, to see how this split structures the autobiographical drive and by extension, how the autobiographical drive finds different generic forms.

I have made no attempt to view Naipaul's writings in light of Caribbean literature as a whole, nor am I primarily concerned here with the ideological implications of the conditions I am describing.[20] I do, however, believe that the underlying structure I am showing and its relation to literary form does serve to situate Naipaul squarely in the broader cultural picture. Abdul R. JanMohamed sees Naipaul as having been "inducted . . . to fulfill the author-function of the colonialist writer."[21] Rob Nixon views his meditations on the state of exile as a pose.[22] My own claim for Naipaul is that the force of self-building which underlies much of his writing is not unlike that of many of his peers in the Caribbean and elsewhere who have had to contend with the conflicting pulls of a Western colonial education and a past which must be accommodated. He too is a post-colonial. The differences in intellectual choices do not change that fact. Moreover, through his singular use of the autobiography mode Naipaul affords us an insight into the ways the postmodern and the post-colonial can converge. This topic, although properly outside the scope of this study, is taken up briefly in the Conclusion.

Finally, having outlined my concept of self and its relation to the production of text in the case of Naipaul's literary oeuvre, I must define the third side of my triangle, my use of the concept of autobiography.

Probably no other genre has undergone as intense a scrutiny and revision of conceptualization in recent decades as autobiography. This is not surprising in light of the fact that the three components of autobiography—self, history and writing—are three of the most thoroughly radicalized concepts in post-structuralist thinking. My treatment of Naipaul's relationship to autobiography is by no means intended as an in-depth study of autobiography theory but is rather a perspective through which I wish to gain a greater insight into one of the shaping forces of Naipaul's oeuvre. Nevertheless, I believe that it is precisely the postmodern undoing of accepted tenets regarding self and history and the consequent destabilizing of boundaries between genres that has served Naipaul for the shaping of his post-colonial self.

For the purposes of my discussion, I will range studies on autobiography between two poles that mirror the tensions inherent in Naipaul's quest for selfhood through autobiography: history and self. I would suggest, as have in different ways William Spengemann and James Olney,[23] that theorists of autobiography can be grouped under two main approaches:

those for whom autobiography is by its very definition bound up with extra-referentiality, a relation, howsoever problematic it may be, between a self and a set of events occurring historically in time;[24] and those who see autobiography as an extension of philosophical questions regarding the ontology of self, or as the scene of self-writing in which extra-referentiality is secondary or even absent altogether.[25] In the first group I am also including what Peter Abbott calls the "promising alternative" which "has been to abandon formal definition altogether and to recast autobiography not as a form but as an act. Here the landmark study is Elizabeth Bruss's *Autobiographical Acts*."[26] In this group, all definitions hinge to a large extent on a truth intention, a stance that relies on what Abbott calls "a proposed identity of writer and subject," which, he states, "cancels the fictional act and ties the narrative to time and this life."[27] For the second group, however, the emphasis on the ontology and evolution of self has rendered the distinctions between the fictional and non-fictional representation irrelevant. Fictional autobiographies become simply one possible mode of self representation.[28] A middle, bridging position between these groups is taken by theorists such as Paul John Eakin in his book *Fictions in Autobiography*.[29] It is not his intention, he argues, "to expel truth from the house of autobiography and to install fiction in its stead."[30] But, acknowledging those twentieth-century autobiographers who "readily accept the proposition that fictions and the fiction-making process are a central constituent of the truth of any life as it is lived,"[31] he concludes that: ". . . the self that is the center of all autobiographical narrative is necessarily a fictive structure," and that "Autobiography in our time is increasingly understood as both an art of memory and an art of the imagination; indeed, memory and imagination become so intimately complementary in the autobiographical act that it is usually impossible for autobiographers and their readers to distinguish between them in practice."[32] It is this intellectual self-consciousness, of which he fully partakes, that provides the grounds for Naipaul's evolution towards selfhood.

Finally, one of the questions remaining unanswered in my study is the extent to which the "drive for autobiography" conditions all of Naipaul's writings. Are the works I have studied representative or singular in what they show? While it is impossible to answer this question adequately within the scope of this study, it is important to point out that no author's oeuvre falls into neat precise patterns. What is explicit in some works is latent or even denied in others. Nevertheless, it is my argument that through the works I have chosen to discuss I am tracing a tangible aspect of Naipaul's writing impetus. The choice of works was made with a double purpose: to study works written in different modes so as to demonstrate how the forms are intrinsic to the problem of writing autobiography, and, at the same time, to space the works chronologically at certain junctures on a continuum that can take into account not only the original split but also Naipaul's development towards a resolution.

CHAPTER ONE

A House for Mr Biswas

In his book *The Forms of Autobiography* William Spengemann makes a case for seeing autobiographical fiction as the last stage in the historical evolution of the genre of autobiography. Any current definition, he says, must extend the notion of autobiography as self-biography, i.e., "a factual account of the writer's own life," to include all those "poems, novels and plays . . .—all of which significantly, are either modern or else particularly susceptible for modernist interpretation—(which) do seem, despite the fictiveness, to address the same problems of self definition that have taxed autobiographers ever since Augustine discovered that the self is a hard ground to plough."[1] Whether or not one agrees that "self definition" is a sufficient criterion by which to define autobiography, it cannot be denied that the autobiographical novel, especially where the emerging self is a writing self, is a powerful and ubiquitous form among the early works of many nineteenth and twentieth century writers, and that the majority of these novelists did not produce, in addition, an autobiography in the traditional sense of the word. It is the claim of this chapter that as a young writer, still believing that he could find a place for himself as an heir to Dickens, Thackeray, etc., the channel for Naipaul's quest for self definition was indeed the autobiographical novel, and that *A House for Mr Biswas*[2] constitutes a deflection of that drive.[3]

A House for Mr Biswas, as noted in the Introduction, was Naipaul's fourth book and the culminating work of his early phase which consisted of works written in the novel or story form and drawing on Trinidadian and Hindu materials to create the fictional world.[4] As such it embodies contradictory impulses. As a body of writing, it is a thwarted attempt, begun, ostensibly, with the embarkation on the writing career, to create a self through the means of the word, what Spengemann has described as "a fictive action, some ground upon which conflicting aspects of the writer's own nature might be reconciled in complete being."[5] At the same time, in its theme, it traces the formation of a split and its accompanying loss of a myth of origin which make the emergence of a self impossible. Although displaced onto a fictional biography of the life of his father, these themes play out Naipaul's own predicament, and ultimately the book confirms what was becoming apparent to Naipaul himself by the time the book was written: that the life-as-English-novelist, i.e., an existence in the borrowed symbolic order could not alone furnish self.

The double, contradictory focus of *A House for Mr Biswas* is presented, not accidentally, through the fictionalized figure of the writer's father, who is the protagonist of the novel.[6] Naipaul himself is recognizable in a secondary, though increasingly important, role as Mr Biswas's son, standing in the wings, interacting with the main character, but ultimately disappearing out of the world of the novel. The concentration of the novel on the figure of the father serves several functions: a) It removes, on the surface, the "autobiographical" onus from the writer, i.e., it seems to declare: "This is not about me, so it cannot really be counted as an autobiographical novel," and b) It affords the reader a double vision: Mr Biswas is read either simply, as a character in a novel in whom we recognize certain aspects of the author himself, or as the prototype of Naipaul's real father, and Anand, the son, as Naipaul himself. Through this displacement a contradictory effect is created: on the one hand the autobiographical impact is deflected, on the other it is doubled—Mr Biswas is both father and son. Thus, while *A House for Mr Biswas* cannot be regarded as an autobiographical novel in the traditional sense, as the figure representing the author is not only not the main protagonist but is somehow kept in the shadows, it is the autobiographical novel par excellence in that it traces the author's split self and loss of myth of origin from his father to its repetition in himself.

The first part of this chapter focuses on the thematization of the split and loss of origin in the character of Mr Biswas as both the source and the doubling of Naipaul's own cultural dislocation, while the second part examines the role of Anand, Naipaul's son, in the thwarted autobiographical act.

Mr Biswas as Father and Son

A character of astonishing, endearing and infuriating lack of worldliness, Mr Biswas has been variously described as "an anti-hero moving through dimension after dimension of nearly epic absurdity,"[7] an offshoot of "a long British novelistic tradition,"[8] and, conversely, the hero of "A Hindu fable, in which the protagonist is finally, despite all the ironies, a positive Hindu hero, and he is cremated according to Hindu rites."[9] The above descriptions are not mutually exclusive, as they capture either one or both sides of what have generally been seen as opposing worlds in the novel.[10] In my analysis of *A House for Mr Biswas* these opposing worlds are represented as a psyche split between the symbolic order and a quest for a vanished past.

I.

Underlying all of Mohun Biswas's wanderings from the time he is orphaned in childhood and taken on by his maternal aunt, Tara, through his abortive stints as a pundit's apprentice, a helper in a rumshop and a sign painter, through marriage with Shama, and being sucked up into the Tulsi family, through his jobs as store keeper at the Chase, a driver on the Tulsi Green Vale estate, to his breakdown and departure to Port of Spain, his venture into journalism, life in Port of Spain, Shorthills and back to Port of Spain, to his appointment as a civil servant and finally back to journalism—underlying all these picaresque wanderings are two themes. The first is an exploration of the relation of the word to reality and history—its power to order reality as opposed to its inadequacy to express the self—as part of Mr Biswas's development in the symbolic order of the written word. The second is the yearning for a house, the quest for place, which is the repeated demand of the lost part of the self, origin, to be accounted for and appeased. Both quests end in failure. The creation of an integrated self is impossible. The fictional "reality" in which these two powerful, insisting forces meet (i.e., Mr Biswas's life among the Tulsis, his marriage, his relationship with his children) appears as a temporary, makeshift state of existence.

The development of the two main themes in the novel is parallel but distinct, and they arise from the death of the protagonist's father which he, Mr Biswas, inadvertently causes. From the very outset, Mr Biswas's life is marked by the double pull of the word. He emerges, we are told, into this world "six-fingered, and born in the wrong way" (p. 15). This unfortunate occurrence causes the midwife to prophesy that "this boy will eat up his own mother and father" (p. 16). And the pundit, consulting his astrological almanac, warns the parents to keep the boy away from water as a means of circumventing the effects of his sixth finger. What kind of water? "'One has to interpret what the book says,'" remarks the pundit. "'And when the book says water, I think it means water in its natural form. . . . I mean . . . keep him away from rivers and ponds'" (p. 17). The prediction comes true with a vengeance: Mr Biswas indirectly causes the death of his father by water. And it is in these contradictory views of the word that the novel is situated: the word is interpreted to give meaning to reality, and the word has magical powers to create and order reality.

The drowning of the father, the major event of Mr Biswas's early life, precipitates the split movement of the novel. Mr Biswas the child, having neglected his duties to guard a neighbour's calf, hides from his family to escape their wrath. His father, Raghu, thinking that the boy has drowned, jumps into the water to save him and is drowned himself. At the same time, Mr Biswas is discovered by his sister, Dehuti, who, thinking that she has seen a ghost, becomes incoherent with screaming and Mr Biswas himself, becoming even more frightened, retreats further into his hiding place (incidentally, under his father's bed). The events he has caused seem to have overwhelmed him altogether in their importance. Here too, contrasting powers of the word are reflected. The father's conviction that the boy has drowned stems from the pundit's decree that he stay away from water. But his interpretation of the pundit's interpretation is wrong—it is he who is fated to die by water, thus fulfilling the other prediction, of the boy who "will eat up his mother and father." At the same time, in the crucial encounter between Mr Biswas and his sister, which might have averted the disaster, words fail both of them.

From a boy destined for the grass-gang, who "would never become a driver or weigher because he wouldn't be able to read. . . " (p. 23), Mr Biswas, as a result of his orphanhood, is taken on by Tara, his aunt; is estranged from his mother Bipti and his brothers; and becomes the recipient of the beginnings of an education—an English culture education, the result of the colonial times. Thus, it is the symbolic killing of his father, and reading and writing that sever him from the old order of things, from what would have become his myth of origin, making him, in the words of the novel, "a wanderer with no place he could call his own" (p. 40), but also initiate him into the realm of the word, the symbolic order, which, through the accession to the Name-of-the-Father, is a means of grounding himself in the social order, culture and history. Unfortunately, the culture and history he tries to adopt are not his own, and colonialism thus becomes the instrument of the loss of origin.

Here a theoretical digression is necessary. The theme of the killing of the father is a complex one. In Freud, the desire to kill the father is a fantasy which is not played out in real life. The child, in the resolution of the Oedipus complex, overcomes his rivalry with his father by identifying with him and relinquishing his desire for the mother, or at least displacing it onto other objects.[11] In Lacan's writings, the Oedipal period signals the process of the child taking his place in the symbolic register of language. Anika Lemaire puts it thus: "The resolution of the Oedipus liberates the subject by giving him, with his Name, a place in the family constellation, an original signifier of self and subjectivity. It promotes him in his realization of self through participation in the world of culture, language and civilization."[12] The death of the father in both theories has special relevance for our text. In *Totem and Taboo*,[13] Freud uses the Oedipal theory to explain the beginnings of civilization, and postulates that the beginning of society as we know it, the fraternal clan as opposed to the patriarchal horde, came into being as the result of the killing and devouring of a horde father by a band of young, displaced sons. Leaving aside for the moment the implications of this speculation for totemism, taboo and religion, what is important to note is that Freud suggests that the structure and organization of society, its laws and strictures, including its sexual limitations, are the outcome of the realization of the Oedipal fantasy of patricide. In *A House for Mr Biswas*, too, the "killing" of the father (and in a symbolic reading I do not think it is important whether this is a real killing or an accidental death) suggests that rather than taking his place in the continuity of the tribe, which would have come about through identification, Mr Biswas is embarking on a beginning that harks back to a kind of cultural primacy, for Freud's theory invokes the point where the cultural and individual converge and become inseparable.[14]

In the writings of Lacan, the killing of the father, together with the whole Oedipal constellation, assumes a symbolic status. According to Lemaire, in Lacan the power of the Law is based on two things: the Forbidden and Sacrifice. Sacrifice, Lemaire says,

> is realized in the Oedipus through the symbolic castration [of the child by the father] which legislates the use of the sex through the death of the father by the fact of his accession to the place of the other: this is the paternal metaphor. We know that the word is the murder of the thing and that this death is the condition of the symbol.[15]

To Lacan, then, the symbolic death of the father is a necessary condition to accession to the paternal metaphor, the Name-of-the-Father: "In the course of the Oedipal phenomenon, the child gains access to the Law . . . by symbolizing the paternal reality, by acceding, that is, to the 'paternal metaphor'."[16] Lemaire goes on to paraphrase Edmond Ortigues:

> The Oedipus, in the broad sense, is radically other and constitutes the fundamental structural moment in the history of a subject. Its articulations are conveyed by the cultural structures of societies, by language, and it is by entering into these that the subject lives them. . . . It is through language that he will progressively assume the

> Oedipal drama from the inside, as an ancestral heritage in which he situates himself before there is any possibility of the act of becoming aware.[17]

For Lacan, the accession into the symbolic, the intervention of the father, the Law, is possible only if the mother recognizes his speech: "If, then, the father is recognized by the mother both as a man and as a representative of the Law, the subject will have access to the 'Name-of-the-Father' or 'paternal metaphor' (Name-of-the-Father, the signifier of the paternal function or installation of the father in the place of the Other, the symbolic order), which gives the symbolic law of the family its basis."[18]

In *A House for Mr Biswas*, the father must be killed not only to allow entrance into the symbolic order but also because the only possible symbolic order available under the political and cultural conditions of the time is not congruent with the father's speech; it is alien and foreign—English culture and language. The father's heritage, the lost and dislocated Hindu civilization, is repudiated.

At the same time, Mr Biswas's "ridding" himself of his father is experienced as incorporation, an act of devouring which suggests that the rejection of the father is as much an assimilation on a primary narcissistic level: "There was also a strange taste in his mouth: he had never eaten meat, but now he felt he had eaten raw white flesh; nauseating saliva rose continually at the back of his throat and he had to keep on spitting, until Tara said: 'What's the matter with you? Are you pregnant?'" (p. 32). The subsequent lifelong irritable stomach Mr Biswas suffers from is a constant reminder of the existence of the cannibalized father.[19]

The juncture of the death of Mr Biswas's father precipitates not only the initiation into the alien symbolic order but also the corresponding, inseparable condition of loss of the pre-verbal world, coupled in Mr Biswas's case with the loss of a compensatory myth of origin, the cultural heritage. This double lack is displaced in the novel onto a severance from land, from place, followed by an obsessive quest for a house: "And so Mr Biswas came to leave the only house to which he had some right. For the next thirty-five years he was to be a wanderer with no place he could call his own, with no family except that which he was to attempt to create out of the engulfing world of the Tulsis" (p. 40).

Interestingly, while the image of the house serves to incorporate the displacement of the loss both of history/place and of primal mother, as shall be discussed on the following pages, the attitude to the figure of the mother herself in the novel contributes further to the structure of the split. A victim of the usurper father, she is alternately viewed as unnurturing and helpless or as an idealized fantasy figure.[20]

The two main themes give rise to two sorts of mental activity in the novel. One is Mr Biswas's attempt to bridge between the symbolic order of the word and reality, to make the life created in the symbolic order *the* reality and to ignore the rest, an attempt which is ultimately unsuccessful because it excludes a myth of origin. The other is his preoccupation with different levels of history making, to bridge the gulf between the symbolic order and the void, the repressed. In a passage between the leaving of the land and the new life at Tara's (p. 41), the narrator remarks that in later life, Mr Biswas as journalist returns to the area of his birth to report on the newly discovered oil—black gold. On his return to this area he discovers that all traces of his past have been obliterated (ironically, his mother's land is now worth a fortune), whereas the article he writes is entitled: "Raleigh's Dream Comes True—'But the Gold is Black. Only the Earth is Yellow. Only the Bush is Green'" (p. 41). Here Mr Biswas, the journalist, recorder of facts for posterity, relates Trinidadian reality to English history (in its most romantic aspect) while acknowledging that it has overrun, swallowed his own personal history.[21] "His grandparents' house had also disappeared .... His navel string, buried on that inauspicious night, and his sixth finger, buried not long after, had turned to dust" (p. 41). And what is true in the case of Mr Biswas's actual physical place in the world is expanded in the narrative to include his inner space.

Related to this theme is the issue of creating and interpreting history. At the funeral of Mr Biswas's father, a photograph is taken of the family of the dead man, which remains the only record of Mr Biswas's childhood until his father's death. Of this photograph it is said, "Mr Biswas never owned a copy of the photograph and he did not see it until 1937, when it made its appearance, framed in passepartout, on the wall of the drawing room of Tara's fine new house at Pagotes" (p. 34). This passage is of interest for several reasons: the photograph is the only "historical document" of Mr Biswas's existence at the time of his father's death and his departure from his place of birth, and 1937 is the only proper date given in the novel. (Mr Biswas's age is not mentioned until the second half of the novel, when he goes to Port of Spain, and happenings in the novel are only very casually and tenuously related to world events, such as the Second World War.) The date 1937, moreover, serves no function at all in relating events to external history, especially as it is not mentioned again on the actual occasion of Mr Biswas seeing the photograph. Both the date and the photograph problematize the position of one's personal history vis-a-vis collective history, the first by being a tangible presence of a vanished existence, and the second by suggesting an unexplained connection between personal, fictional and historical events.

Thus through the indirect act of killing his father and its immediate ramifications, we have an important juncture of the major themes of the novel, the threshold of an internal split in Mr Biswas: the life in the symbolic register, a losing struggle to inhabit the word in order to create and recreate personal history, i.e., to recover origin, and the obliteration or repression of the past and the abandonment of place for a life of wandering and rootlessness.

II.

The parallel threads, life in the word and the quest for a house/place, converge twice in the novel: once at the end of Part One in the Green Vale episode, i.e., almost exactly in the middle of the work, and again at the end of the book when Mr Biswas finally builds his house on Sikkim Street, only to die in it. What I have been calling Mr Biswas's "life in the word" is developed along two main axes: the absorption and interpretation of the written word, as in books, documents, etc., in order to comprehend reality and interact with it, and the creative use of the word in the attempt to construct self. The tracing of that development necessitates a certain linearity of reading, as the following pages demonstrate.

The first event which befalls Mr Biswas in his new life after the death of his father, his introduction into the symbolic order, is his being issued with a birth certificate. An invented birth date and a paper that states the fact of his birth declare his previous existence in the world null and void and establish his entrance into the new order: "In this way official notice was taken of Mr Biswas's existence and he entered the new world" (p. 44). But in this new world, at school, for example, what he learns, together with some unreal facts about reality which he is unable to apply to himself, is that "ought oughts are ought" (p. 44)—that nothing comes of nothing. This equation becomes for him, as it will for Naipaul, the essence of his existence—the void at the centre turns all subsequent activity into nought.

The initial meaninglessness of the symbolic order he has entered creates a diversion in Mr Biswas which is to last into his adulthood and serves as his first attempt to use the word as an expression of self. Rather than puzzle out the meaning of the symbols he is learning, he becomes enamored with their shape, which has the power to overcome their external reference. In one instance, he decorates the word "cancelled" which he has written across his answers to an exam, and by giving the letters a distinctive shape and colour, he effectively belies the meaning of "cancelled." In another, commanded to write "I am an ass" on the blackboard, "Mr Biswas outlined stylish, contemptuous letters, and the class tittered approvingly" (p. 47). In a world where the word ties in with no inner meaning, Mr Biswas concentrates on the form.

At the same time, written words have the power to create reality, to order it and to influence it. His birth certificate reads: "Father's occupation. Labourer," and, the narrator notes, ". . . throughout life his position was like that. As one of the Tulsi sons-in-law and as a journalist he found himself among people with money and sometimes with graces . . . but always, at the end, he returned to his crowded shabby room" (p. 49).

As his life embarks on a series of episodic abortive trials at jobs and dwelling places, Mr Biswas engages on a voyage of self-education. It is still the strange English or rather Western culture, but he slowly becomes more at home in it. He begins by reading to his uncle Ajodha from *Bell's Standard Elocutionist* with its poem "Bingen on the Rhine," and continues with the exploration of the *Book of Comprehensive Knowledge* discovered on Ajodha's veranda. These are followed by novels and romances, and later by the writings of Marcus Aurelius whose influence becomes lifelong, his philosophy a mainstay and comfort. The randomness of the selection and the distortion it undoubtedly produces concerning Western culture highlight the problematics of inhabiting an alien culture.

A serious quarrel with Tara and Bipti over events in the rum shop brings about Mr Biswas's final rift with his mother and her house and leads him into the first occupation which relates directly to a creative relationship with the word—a sign painter. "He thought R and S the most beautiful of Roman letters; no letter could express so many moods as R, without losing its beauty; and what could compare with the swing and rhythm of S?" (p. 76). Sign painting also attracts Mr Biswas because of the slogan-like nature of signs, yet another relation of the word to truth and history. All signs are slogans (as are newspaper headlines, as we shall see): they at once capture the essence of the message, and depersonalize it by removing it from the context of the signified. Throughout his life Mr Biswas remains particularly vulnerable to slogans of all kinds. They seduce him with their self-confidence and absolutism, but they also allow him to avoid looking inward.

Another dismal attempt on the part of Mr Biswas to apply the lessons of the written word to reality stems from the desire for romance and love as represented in Western novels and romances. A note that he writes to Shama, a daughter of the rich Tulsi family: "I love you and want to talk to you," is intercepted and leads to his very unromantic marriage and engulfment in the world of the Tulsis. The power of the written word here is immense. At no time during the entire marriage proceedings is there anything to force Mr Biswas to go through with it. But, as with his birth certificate and many other written texts which appear in this narrative, the words both assume the authority of a decree and foreshadow, even prophesy, events in the lives of the protagonists. And yet, when speaking to his friend Alec, the sign painter, Mr Biswas offers yet another version of the events: "Well, I see this girl, you know. I see this girl and she was looking at me, and I was looking at she. So I give she a little of the old sweet talk and I see that she was liking me too. And, well, to cut a long story short, I ask to see the mother" (pp. 92–93). For Mr Biswas it is of the utmost importance to be in control, to shape his own life but his success at it is in reverse proportion to his desire. All his life he oscillates between being completely under the sway of the word and attempting to use it to create a self.

As Mr Biswas lives a life of pulverized son-in-law and husband in the Tulsi house, he slowly develops into language, the English language which he hopes can give meaning to reality. During this time, it is noted, Mr Biswas "nearly always spoke English at Hanuman House, even when the other person spoke Hindi; it had become one of his principles" (pp. 118–119).

From sign painting, the preoccupation with the outer form of the signifier, Mr Biswas begins a tentative play with the possibilities of meaning itself. Pankaj Rai, an Aryan preacher, is Mr Biswas's first real exposure to the process of using words creatively. Misir, Mr Biswas's journalist friend, proclaims Pankaj Rai to be a purist. "Mr Biswas had not asked what a purist was, but the word, pronounced with reverence by Misir, appealed strongly to him, suggesting not only purity and fastidiousness, but also elegance and breeding" (p. 116).

Mr Biswas discovers the power of giving meaning to a word:

> Purist, Mr Biswas thought, when he saw Pankaj Rai. The man *is* a purist. He was elegant in a long, black, close-fitting Indian coat; and when he shook Mr Biswas by the hand, Mr Biswas surrendered to his graciousness at the same time noting with satisfaction that Pankaj Rai was as short as himself and had an equally ugly nose (p. 116).

Mr Biswas "incorporates" the term "purist" into his vocabulary: "He spoke without flourish, and slowly, as if tasting the phrases beforehand, like a good purist; and it was a revelation to Mr

Biswas that words and phrases which by themselves were commonplace, could be welded into sentences of such balance and beauty. He found he agreed with everything Pankaj Rai said . . . " (p. 116).

After the speech, Pankaj Rai autographs his book for Mr Biswas: "He wrote Mr Biswas's name as well, describing him as a 'dear friend'. Below this inscription Mr Biswas wrote: 'Presented to Mohun Biswas by his dear friend Pankaj Rai, B A L L B'" (pp. 116–117). Thus Mr Biswas learns to use the word to make a reality and to give himself an identity, but also to shelter behind it, to colour the real world. The autograph itself reflects both the lack of authenticity, the fraudulence of the written word and, again, its power to influence reality.

At the Chase, Mr Biswas becomes acquainted with the power and the helplessness of the word, trying to make it do what he wants and usually failing. A few examples will suffice. The Chase is where the villager's continue to call the store the "Tulsi shop" despite Mr Biswas's newly painted sign which reads: THE BONNE ESPERANCE GROCERY: M Biswas, Prop., Goods at City Prices. It is while he is at the Chase that his daughter is born and named Savi by the pundit, against his will, and he is unable to impose the name he has chosen on the world of Hanuman House. Furthermore, Savi's birth certificate states: "Occupation of father. Labourer" (p. 163), which, of course, repeats his own birth certificate and at the same time reinforces a stigma which he cannot combat.

On the other hand, Misir, his journalist friend, is trying his hand at short stories, tragic tales about the mockery fate makes of man, about the elusive nature of luck which is always snatched away from man at the last moment or turned against him. In these stories, the hero always makes the wrong decision at the very moment his luck is about to change, thus subverting any possibility of having effective control over his life. An uncanny foreshadowing of Mr Biswas's life at the Chase and the troubles he gets into there a little later on, Misir's stories also seem to belong to those narratives in the novel which have the power to suggest if not make the future.

Mr Biswas's own attempts to write stories are unsuccessful: "But Mr Biswas could never devise a story, and he lacked Misir's tragic vision; whatever his mood, and however painful his subject, he became irreverent and facetious as soon as he began to write" (p. 183). Here begins another recurring motif: the illusory notion of fiction as expressive of the deepest part of the self, and the gap between it and other forms of writing. Mr Biswas, at this point, is unable to harness words to create a fictive reality which he feels would express his deepest self.

III.

The quest for a past in the shape of a house, the parallel underlying theme of the narrative, is unceasing and unremitting in its intensity throughout the novel and acts as a counterpart to the activity in the symbolic order: "He had lived in many houses. And how easy it was to think of those houses without him! . . . And even more remote, that house of mud and grass in the swamplands: probably pulled down now and ploughed up. Beyond that a void. There was nothing to speak of him" (pp. 131–132).

Whether we regard the house as a symbol of the body, symbolizing the desire for the mother,[22] or as a "Bachelardian" place in the imagination where we dream of primal shelter and belonging,[23] a house here is a rooting into place, a return to an original state of belonging, of communing with the self, and for Mr Biswas a return to the lost childhood, self, and, ultimately, death. The quest for a house is the underside of his advancement in the symbolic sphere, an unceasing demand, a pull back to the pre-verbal, the protective wholeness. As such, it is repetitious and undeveloping (as opposed to the accession into the written word which is a dynamic process). It is also doomed to fail because the primary desire behind it is unappeasable, and because Mr Biswas never succeeds (except on one occasion) in bridging the gap between the two parts of himself.

The novel opens with a prologue which is in fact an epilogue recounting the buying of the house on Sikkim Street and Mr Biswas's death soon after. Ultimately, the acquisition of the past in this novel, the coming full circle back to the beginning, is a return to death.[24] To live is to be without past and hence self. This state of existence is uncannily repeated in *The Enigma of Arrival*, written twenty-five years later, only there, as will be seen, the autobiographical act becomes possible through the self-conscious creation of a myth of origin.

And yet, the beauty and complexity of the house symbol is that the house, as opposed to the word—a signifier—is a concrete thing, a structure, a place, a material being whose presence in reality is an incontrovertible fact. The quest for a house, from this viewpoint, is an attempt to be grounded in reality, to render concrete that void, the absence of origin, the inexpressible, which is at the centre of existence. Whether a house stands or falls depends entirely on the materials of which it is made and the workmanship invested in its building. To have a house is for all intents and purposes to be a house, to have an irrefutable existence. The two spheres, the void and the symbolic, meet but do not overlap in the reality of the novel. On the one hand is the pull of the void translated as a need to concretize existence, on the other is the symbolic order, a realm through which reality may be apprehended and controlled. Mr Biswas tries to alleviate the pain of his constant failure to have/be a house through the acquiring of a symbolic existence. This, however, cannot be achieved through a borrowed culture—it cannot ultimately be related back to his "house." For Mr Biswas, most of "life" is an unbridgeable dichotomy between writing, which in itself comprises many levels, and being. There is only one occasion in the narrative when a continuous thread is established from primal "house" to writing—the poem he writes about his mother after her death, which links with a number of elusive experiences of the past, forming a delicate thematic thread. But even there the results are not unequivocal.

Mr Biswas's struggles against fragmentation and disintegration and his attempts at organization out of chaos are poignantly rendered through the description of the various items of furniture which accompany the family on their wanderings. The bits and pieces must be squeezed into the given space of each temporary dwelling much like the reality, desires, information, etc., that are constantly being rearranged in his inner space.

Associated with the quest for a house as a displacement for lost origin are episodes of intangible memories of a real vanished past. At the Chase, the debtor against whom Mr Biswas takes action is Mungroo, the leader of the village stick-fighters, and a man Mr Biswas admires for keeping Hindu tradition and heritage alive. The ritual of making the sticks for the fights evokes in Mr Biswas a deep-seated, non-verbal memory of his father and an accompanying sense of tradition:

> There was no scent as pleasant as that of barely roasted *poui*: faint, yet so lasting it seemed to come from afar, from some immeasurable depth captive within the wood: as faint as the scent of the *pouis* Raghu roasted in the village like this, in a yard like this, in a bonfire like this: bringing sensations, not pictures, of an evening meal being cooked over a fire that shone on a mud wall.... Sensations as faint as the scent of the *poui* itself, but sadly evanescent, refusing to be seized or to be translated into a concrete memory (p. 174).

The beauty of the description, the motif of repetition and continuity, are enhanced by the language: the repetition of the words "like this," the repetition of sounds in "scent" and "evanescent," and the delicacy of the phrasing. This is the first of a number of moments occurring on rare occasions throughout his life in which the sense of the past, going back beyond his own individual experience to encompass a vanished world, is apprehended directly, however tenuously, through sensation.

IV.

The episode of Green Vale, the next stop in Mr Biswas's wanderings, heralds the major turning point in the book both in terms of plot and in terms of theme. At Green Vale the gulf between Mr Biswas's quest for a house and the realm of the word—the acquired symbolic realm—reaches intolerable proportions, resulting in a breaking down of boundaries between the real world and the world of fear and fantasy. It is also the point where the two parallel strands, the word and place, converge.

At Green Vale all the forces pressing on Mr Biswas finally erupt. First, the written word becomes a trap, a prison which blocks rather than facilitates his interaction with external reality. In the makeshift barracks, the side window (the extra privilege of an end-room) is nailed shut and plastered over with newspapers: "Its position could only be guessed at, since newspaper covered the walls from top to bottom. This had obviously been the work of a literate. No sheet was placed upside down, and Mr Biswas found himself continuously exposed to the journalism of his time, its bounce and excitement bottled and made quaint in these old newspapers" (p. 206).

Mr Biswas is locked within the framework of the barracks room, and the newspapers plastered on the wall, especially one lead sentence, come to obsess his mind: "Amazing scenes were witnessed yesterday when" (p. 211). The sentence, in this context, captures the gap between the written word and Mr Biswas's world, or between the signifier and the signified, at this time: the sentence is not complete—the words suggest a magical relation to reality which is either inexpressible, or, for Mr Biswas, inaccessible. Mr Biswas does not have the words, nor has he witnessed the amazing scenes with which to complete the sentence. Either his reality is too futile or he has not yet learned how to use the power of the word to order reality, to make a scene amazing. In addition, the "witnessing of a scene" conjures up the "primal scene," a witnessing which cannot be completed, which may indeed never have taken place, but which is a crucial determiner of the present.

At the same time, Mr Biswas begins to letter "religious tags on strips of cardboard, which he hung on the walls against the newspapers. . . . He who believeth in me of him I will never lose hold and he shall never lose hold of me" (p. 211). This other source of the word—Scripture—poses another possibility of grounding reality, based on a different kind of "witnessing," on faith. Neither option—the use of the word to render reality with substance, magic, or its use to achieve faith in something beyond reality, can save Mr Biswas now as they are divorced from meaning and reduced to slogans. The stifling boredom and futility of his life, the estrangement of his family, the hostility of the workers under him, and above all, his own alienation from the whole of this reality, precipitate a descent into a void, a descent which not only brings to a climax the themes of house and language which I have been tracing, but which also weaves in the layers of repetition in the relationship between Mr Biswas and Anand his son, and to some extent his daughter Savi.

In his desperation to make a connection between himself and the surrounding world, Mr Biswas first tries to make Savi part of his world, to "claim" her in his words, and when that fails, he tries the same with Anand, his son. His first act is to buy Savi a doll's house for Christmas. Besides constituting an obvious projection of his own yearning, the doll's house is also a way of providing Savi with a symbolic individual identity. It is precisely this kind of assertion of self which cannot be tolerated at Hanuman House and Shama, torn between living with tradition and her loyalty to Mr Biswas, destroys the house to keep the peace.

Savi, we are told, during this episode, knew that the Christmas signs hung in the Tulsi store were painted by her father:

> Savi knew, and was proud, that the signs had been done by her father. But their gaiety puzzled her; she couldn't associate them with the morose man she went to see in the dingy barrackroom and who sometimes came to see her. She felt, with a sense of loss that became sharper as Christmas drew nearer, that the signs had been done at some time beyond her memory when her father lived happily at Hanuman House with her mother and everyone else (p. 212).

For Savi, then, Mr Biswas's painted signs suggest a time of cohesion and harmony from which she sprang, just as for Mr Biswas the scent of the *poui* evoked sensations of an unremembered time of security in childhood. Though Mr Biswas's signifiers are words, i.e., on a "higher" scale than *poui* sticks, it is not their meaning which Savi absorbs but their shape and colour. The world they summon up is the world of the senses. Furthermore, the past which is thus evoked is idealized and contaminated by the shape, colour and smell associated with the signifiers. Mr Biswas never lived happily at Hanuman House, and his parents lived in poverty and discord (at the time of his birth his mother ran away to her parents). Savi, and later Anand, repeat in their own lives the yearning for a vanished, idealized past. The question which the text thus raises, and which becomes a central issue in subsequent works, is that of the status of the past—real or fantasized, fiction or truth? In his struggle against the forces closing in on him, in his sense of losing the battle of the survival of his separate being, a new process begins for Mr Biswas. In his room, alone, imprisoned among his quotations,

> he talked to himself, shouted, did everything as noisily as he could. Nothing replied. Nothing changed. *Amazing scenes were witnessed yesterday when*. The newspapers remained as jaunty as they had been, the quotations as sedate. *Of him I will never lose hold and he shall never lose hold of me*. But now in the shape and position of everything around him, the trees, the furniture, even those letters he had made with brush and ink, there was an alertness, an expectancy (p. 228).

The written words, to put it differently, remain as meaningless and unsupporting as they were, whereas the real world slowly turns into animate signifiers of multiple meanings, fears and fantasies. As time passes, the objects around him take on a hitherto undreamt-of meaning:

> The chair fell silent. He looked away from it. On the wall he saw a nail that could puncture his eye. The window could trap and mangle. So could the door. Every leg of the green table could press and crush. . . . He lay face down on the bed, not wanting to see and, to drive out the shapes of objects from his head, he concentrated on the shapes of letters, working out design after design for the letter R (pp. 229–230).

Mr Biswas reverts to the only way he knows to control the word—through the shape of the sign—but this is not sufficient.

The process of disintegration is opposed by a last-ditch attempt at integration, the building of a house: "As soon as he saw the barracks Mr Biswas decided that the time had come for him to build his own house, by whatever means" (p. 206). He commissions Mr Maclean, a builder, to build him a house on an empty Tulsi site, but as his funds dwindle, so the materials used for the house get worse and worse in quality until they are barely usable. Instead of pitchpine for the floor, he gets cedar planks; for rafters he makes do with tree branches; cast off corrugated iron and pitch serve instead of cement to patch the holes in the roof; and when the sun shines the asphalt begins to melt and create "a legion of slim, black, growing snakes" (p. 264) which come to haunt his fantasies. Again, rather than mould reality to fit his fantasies, this house is an example of how the nightmarish aspect of his fantasy of the house is fulfilled.

Instead of the hoped-for haven, the house becomes the harbinger of fear—fear that his house might be burned down, fear of people, fear of the black cloud which threatens to engulf his mind: "Unless he was careful the cloud would funnel into his head" (p. 266). A profound questioning takes hold of him regarding the meaning of his life, the waste of it, the waste of fear. He tries to fend off the encroachment of the void, fear, fantasy, by reading and continuing to decorate his walls. The building of the house progresses, but its basic instability, exemplified by the hanging snakes, pursues him even in his dreams. It is as if this house, the product of his dreams, is not only the fulfillment of the negation of his dream, but is in itself disintegrating into signifiers of his repressed, neurotic fantasies.

This chapter also marks a juncture of Anand's and Mr Biswas's stories. For Mr Biswas it is an end, a void, a pit from which he will emerge as a writer. For Anand, it is the beginning of a new life—of education, of identification with his father, coupled with an alienation leading to a life of solitude and dreams of escape.

During the ensuing storm, Mr Biswas becomes lost to the world, hoping to find relief in "writing with his finger on his head" (p. 288), or reciting the *Sita Rama* endlessly, "always with a look of exasperation." The house is overcome by the force of the wind and rain and the light goes out:

> Then there was a roar that overrode them all. When it struck the house, the window burst open, the light went instantly out, the rain lashed in, the lightning lit up the room and the world outside, and when the lightning went

> out the room was part of the black void. Anand began to scream. He waited for his father to say something, to close the window, light the lamp. But Mr Biswas only muttered on the bed and the rain and wind swept through the room . . . and forced open the door to the drawing-room, wall-less, floorless, of the house Mr Biswas had built (p. 292).

The collapse of the house and the extinguishing of the lamp (to be relit by strangers) have different symbolic meanings for Mr Biswas and Anand. For Mr Biswas the whole episode represents the succumbing to and perhaps recognition of a basic chaos and nothingness which is at the centre of his being. Only the passage through this experience will enable him subsequently to find a habitation in language through a career in journalism, however temporarily and unsatisfactorily. For Anand, on the other hand, the scene is a repetition of Mr Biswas's own childhood. Abandoned at a crucial moment by his father, who undergoes a kind of death, he accepts the light of a stranger. From that moment begins his education away from his past.

V.

From the black void of the non-self Mr Biswas emerges, in the second part of the novel, to a life inhabited almost completely in the word. As the power of the reality of the word seems to grow, so the insistent necessity of finding a house recedes. But it is ultimately the inability to bridge between these two realms that causes the downfall of the hero.

Mohun Biswas comes to Port of Spain literally to seek his fortune.[25] Whatever it is that propels him towards life in the word is determined to keep the problem of past/origin out of sight, i.e., repressed. As he travels towards that city, "he fixed his eyes on a house, as small and as neat as a doll's house, on the distant hills of the Northern Range; . . . The plain fell behind, the mountains grew nearer; but the doll's house remained as small as ever and when the bus turned into the Eastern Main Road Mr Biswas lost sight of it" (p. 308). It is this repression that is the main motivating force of the second part of *A House for Mr Biswas*.

In Port of Spain, looking for a job, Mr Biswas is led almost unconsciously to the office of the *Sentinel* (Misir's old newspaper). There, some inner button seems to be released with tremendous energy. The line with which he was previously obsessed, "Amazing scenes were witnessed yesterday when," and which at the barracks he could not continue, is suddenly and frenetically completed several times in his mind in longer and longer versions: First, "Passers-by stopped and stared yesterday when," going on to: "Amazing scenes were witnessed in St. Vincent Street yesterday when Mohun Biswas, 31 . . . assaulted a receptionist," culminating in the virtually orgiastic: ". . . assaulted a receptionist at the offices of the *Trinidad Sentinel*. People ducked behind desks as Biswas, father of four, walked into the building with guns blazing, shot the editor and four reporters dead, and then set fire to the building . . ." (p. 319).

Although in actual fact Mr Biswas walks in, meets the editor, is given a day's work as a sign painter and then a trial as a journalist, internally something important has fallen into place. His pent-up aggression towards Shama and the children (editor and four reporters shot), his translation of it into a fictive scene in which he is a Western-style, gun-toting hero in control of the situation, its incorporation into a journalistic framework ("Amazing scenes were witnessed," "In an exclusive interview with our special correspondent . . .") create an authentic medium in which Mr Biswas can accede to the symbolic order of the word—living and writing the life of a reporter.

In the kind of journalism encouraged by the editor, Mr Burnett, reality is only a springboard for the imagination to build upon. At first Mr Biswas uses the stories to release his barely concealed aggression and loneliness. A stint as shipping reporter, for example, yields the following item:

> DADDY COMES HOME IN A COFFIN /U.S. Explorer's Last Journey/ ON ICE,/ by M. Biswas./ Somewhere in America in a neat little red-roofed cottage four children ask their mother every day: 'Mummy, when is Daddy coming home?'/ Less than a year ago Daddy—George Elmer Edman, the celebrated traveller and explorer—left home to

> explore the Amazon./ Well, I have news for you, kiddies./ Daddy is on his way home./ Yesterday he passed through Trinidad. In a coffin (p. 327).

The abuse of the "objective" facts notwithstanding, this news item (like other news features that he writes) tells his own story: the lonely hero, a wanderer and an explorer of life who never comes home except in a coffin. Defeat and death in the Amazon, with its connotation of primitive jungles and warring matriarchal societies, recalls Mr Biswas's struggle with Hanuman House ruled by Mrs Tulsi.

Mr Biswas's vocation as reporter is not merely an intellectual fulfillment; it is the attempt to write a life. It is the use of the written word to order a reality, to create an existence. Mr Biswas's acquisition of writing is a cultural acquisition of English and English culture, but it is first and foremost a life-as-writer, life created through writing.

The culmination of this process is apparent in Mr Biswas's role of the Scarlet Pimpernel, a circulation gimmick in which Biswas roams the countryside (echoes of the great explorer) and readers are meant to come up to him and say: "You are the Scarlet Pimpernel and I claim the *Sentinel* prize" (p. 328). Not only is the borrowed personality here a traditional, swashbuckling English hero (not unlike Sir Walter Raleigh) of the time of the French Revolution (undoubtedly suddenly fashionable due to the popularity of the film with Leslie Howard which was released around that time) and the polar opposite to himself, but his photograph appears in the paper daily and he is obliged to make up fantastic stories about his exploits to cover up the failure of the project. Reality and writing merge: his life is the story, and at the same time his story improves and manipulates reality by giving people the opportunity to claim the prize.

That journalism is for Mr Biswas the beginning of the only existence he consciously recognizes and can be active in, a grounding in reality of his self, emerges from the narrative in other ways as well. The beginning of Part Two, with Mr Biswas's arrival in Port of Spain, establishes his age: "Amazing scenes were witnessed yesterday in St. Vincent Street when Mr Biswas, 31, unemployed, of no fixed address, assaulted a receptionist," etc. In all of Part I, regardless of the events being described, Mr Biswas's age is never given. At most it can be approximately surmised. Furthermore, in Part Two, time is measured against reality: ". . . to the City of Port of Spain, where with one short break he was to spend the rest of his life, and where at Sikkim Street he was to die fifteen years later. . ." (p. 307). In Part One, in contrast, time has no meaning, as it leads nowhere. The single date it contains, 1937, seemingly arbitrarily mentioned but in fact referring to an occasion taking place in Part Two, contributes to the sense that Part One takes place in a kind of pre-time.

And yet, as Mr Biswas gains confidence in his new order, it becomes insufficient. It neither touches his inner core, his void, nor does it give meaning to the reality of his family relationships. He constantly searches for new ways of expression. His first try leads him to the absurdities of the Ideal School of Journalism, an English correspondence course, and the writing of essays to order on given topics utilizing "background hints " such as ". . . the tradesmen's blinds, the crack of bat on ball on the village green. . . " or poetic inspiration such as "Autumn is with us again! . . . 'Season of mist and mellow fruitfulness'" (p. 343). Recognizing the grotesqueness of his attempt to be inspired by English countryside, poetry and customs, Mr Biswas sets out once again to write fiction. While journalism, the manipulator of reality, a combination of fact and fantasy, can provide a place of habitation, building blocks of a life, "writing" as in fiction represents for him a "truth," a meaning, something essential, which has its origins in a pre-symbolic time and place.

The fixed opening of all of his stories: "At the age of 33, when he was already the father of four children. . . " (p. 344) comes to obsess him as once the "amazing scenes" headline did, and is just as incompletable. No matter how hard he tries, he can never progress further than a few pages. The hero is himself, a man trapped into marriage, yearning for the love of a young slender, barren, inaccessible girl, in short one who is everything that his wife Shama is not. "He began these stories with joy; they left him dissatisfied and feeling unclean" (p. 345). And whereas it has become possible for Mr Biswas, in journalism, to use the language/writing of an acquired culture, to create a fabricated reality, to fill the role of historian and be a part of that "history," he cannot use the same acquired culture to write his personal history, his truth about the past. He cannot, in other words, get beyond the English to the "Hindi" and all that it implies. For Mr Biswas, then, as for Naipaul, writing is both the only means out of the void, a powerful instrument over reality, and at the same time a barrier against the void which must be penetrated if truth is to be found.

This period of relative peace also constitutes the highest point of equilibrium in Mr Biswas's life, a time when journalism provides a place of habitation which alleviates the pangs of family life, grants a freedom of creation and connects reality to fantasy. However, having achieved a pinnacle of sorts in the inhabitation of the written word, Mr Biswas spends the rest of his life discovering its inadequacies.

The plot offers a range of encounters with different possibilities of manipulating the written word. First, the type of journalism advocated at the *Sentinel* changes, resulting in a different kind of documentation, a different relation to history and reality. At a later stage, Mr Biswas leaves journalism and becomes a civil servant dealing with sociological aspects of the written word. None of these variations gives him the sense of fulfillment accorded him in the early days of journalism; on the contrary, they increase the gap between his inner life and his reality—family life, housing situation—which, despite his passivity, engage a growing part of himself. In no way do they touch the inexpressible core or void. As the gap widens between the symbolic order and reality, Mr Biswas shifts his ambitions to his son, and Anand takes on this legacy with all its complexity and conflicts. The last part of my analysis examines three or four sections which illustrate this process.

Under Mr Burnett's stewardship, Mr Biswas had discovered the intoxication of using language to create a world rather than represent the world. The creation of a world, grounded in real facts, serves Mr Biswas as a symbolic house, but a core of void always remains. However, the blending of fact and fantasy in journalism is, on the surface, at least an umbrella over the void. With the departure of Mr Burnett, the type of reporting required by the paper changes. "Don't be bright, just get it right" (p. 369) the walls scream—a slogan which has the power to deflate Mr Biswas completely. From now on he is expected to report facts and facts alone. "'Write?'" he says to Shama, "'I don't call that writing. Is more like filling up a form . . . '" (p. 370). The unadorned fact has no interest for Mr Biswas. For him truth, or the inhabitation of language, is bound up with creation. It is his own life he is creating while writing. Similarly, a little later, "He didn't write scandalous interviews with one-eyed men: he wrote serious surveys of the work done by the Institute for the Blind . . . . It was his duty to praise . . . He had not so much to distort as to ignore: to forget the bare, toughened feet of the children in an orphanage. . . " (p. 375). The "factual" journalism, it transpires, is no more "truthful" than the sensationalist fantasies he had been concocting before. Furthermore, by not engaging his imagination, his creativity, the new type of journalism only increases the gap between the inhabitation of the written word, reality and inner life.

This drift is exemplified in other ways in the novel. When Mr Burnett leaves, his own paper, the *Sentinel* "reported Mr Burnett's departure on the society page . . . He was reported as being sorry to leave" (p. 369). Other newspapers, which consider the *Sentinel* as a sensationalist muckraker, report that "an Indian troupe, made up of dancers, a fire-walker, a snake-charmer and a man who could rest on a bed of nails [metaphoric allusions to Burnett's attributes] was accompanying Mr Burnett, a former editor of a local newspaper, on his travels to America. One headline was 'The Circus Moves On'" (p. 369). Suffice it to note in this context the power of the word to contaminate reality or to cast doubts on our versions of reality. A few months later Mr Biswas receives a letter from Mr Burnett from America. In this letter, Mr Burnett picks up the theme of circus (had Mr Burnett read those headlines?), and embroiders on it in a humorous vein: "Perhaps fire in Trinidad is different. But when that boy from St. James was given one small American fire to walk through, he just ran. Away. . . . The snake charmer was all right until his snake bit him. . . . " (p. 384). Mr Burnett's bitterness comes through despite his bravado, although, like Mr Biswas, he writes to conceal rather than expose himself. Furthermore, we are told that the stamp on the envelope was cancelled with the words "Report obscene mail to your postmaster" (p. 384). The contiguity of this phrase with Burnett's letter contaminates its message. It becomes in a sense an obscene letter, or perhaps a letter about the obscenity of life. Either way, we are further away from the facts, or truth, or Mr Burnett's actual history, than before. And yet, as a passage in a novel, there is a complexity in it which yields a greater truth than the bare facts possess. Is this Naipaul's own answer to his father's old question?

At Shorthills, a doomed adventure in which the Tulsis make a misguided attempt to return to the land (a symbolic attempt to return to some idealized colonial existence), to halt the inevitable crumbling of old hierarchies and family structure, Mr Biswas uses the last of his savings (once again) to build a house virtually in the jungle. He invites his mother, a long-overdue obligation, to visit, and this duty turns out to provide one of the rare moments in which reality yields an authentic experience for Mr Biswas:

> When, after Bipti's death, Mr Biswas wished to be reminded of her, he thought less of his childhood . . . than of this fortnight at Shorthills. He thought of one moment in particular. . . One afternoon, when he had pushed his bicycle up the earth steps to the top of the hill, he saw that part of the ground, which he had left that morning cumbered and unbroken, had been cleared and levelled and forked. The black earth was soft and stoneless; the spade had cut cleanly into it, leaving damp walls as smooth as mason's work. Here and there the prongs of the fork had left shallow parallel indentations on the upturned earth. In the setting sun, the sad dusk, with Bipti working in a garden that looked, for a moment, like a garden he had known a dark time ages ago, the intervening years fell away. Thereafter the marks of a fork in earth made him think of that moment at the top of the hill, and of Bipti (pp. 426-427).

This moment is linked with the smell of *poui*, with Savi's admiration of her father's hand-painted signs, with the remembered version of Bipti's welcome of him when he returned, misjudged and humiliated, from his trial as a pundit's apprentice, all moments when experience in reality connects with the ineffable past of wholeness, origin, being on the land, of a unity of past and present. It is these moments which Mr Biswas is storing up in order to write his true story. (As a moment in time, however, it is less than temporary—ironically the house burns down during Mr Biswas's firing of the land, an act undertaken to avoid the encroachment of the jungle on his "space.")

Back in Port of Spain, journalism again becomes a double-edged shelter. On the one hand it widens the gap between Mr Biswas's life in the symbolic order and his life in reality, on the other, it is the story of his own life:

> So the *Sentinel* started the Deserving Destitutes Fund, the name suggesting that there was not a necessary inconsistency between the fund and the leaders which spoke of the unemployed as the unemployable . . . Mr Biswas was appointed investigator. It was his duty to read the applications from destitutes, reject the undeserving, visit the others to see how deserving or desperate they were, and then, if the circumstances warranted it, to write harrowing accounts of their plight, harrowing enough to encourage contributions for the fund. He had to find one deserving destitute a day (pp. 440–441).

Mr Biswas is not only writing himself, he is also living his stories. "Day after day he visited the eastern sections of the city where the narrow houses pressed their scabbed and blistered facades together and hid the horrors that lay behind them: . . . Day after day he came upon people so broken, so listless, it would have required the devotion of a lifetime to restore them" (pp. 441–442). The plight of the destitute echoes the difficulties of his own existence and, again, foreshadows the time, several months later, when Mr Biswas and his whole family are moved temporarily into a Tulsi tenement while the big house is readied for Owad's triumphant return from England:

> The wooden walls were unpainted, grey-black, rotting; at every step on the patched, shaky floor wood dust excavated by woodlice showered down; there was no ceiling and the naked galvanized roof was fluffy with soot; there was no electricity. Where would the furniture go? Where would they sleep, cook, wash? Where would the children study? (p. 526).

As the gap between the symbolic order of the word and Mr Biswas's reality widens, another, subtle development is brought to a climax in Mr Biswas's inner reality, one which seems to bring him into contact with his innermost core. Mr Biswas is invited to join a literary group where he feels an outsider because he has written nothing that he feels he can offer. During this same period, his mother dies. Her death oppresses him

> by a sense of loss: not of present loss, but of something missed in the past. . . and always there was the sight of Shama and the children, alien growths, alien affections, which fed on him and called him away from that part of him which yet remained purely himself, that part which had for long been submerged and was now to disappear (p. 480).

The occasion of his mother's death produces two written texts and creates a moment in Mr Biswas's life when a single thread connects all his disparate motifs. One of these texts is a letter to the doctor who had signed Bipti's death certificate and had shown disrespect to his brothers and to Bipti: "They had complained and the doctor had damned them and damned their mother. His bad temper continued all the way to the house; with anger and disrespect he had examined Bipti's body, signed the certificate, demanded his fee and left" (p. 482). Mr Biswas, who had not actually been present at the time, is deeply humiliated by the incident. His mother's death revives all his buried and denied identification with his Hindu background. The disrespect shown is not only human, but ethnic. It also exacerbates his guilt feelings towards his mother whom he feels he had not loved. Mr Biswas composes a letter of eight pages to the doctor in which he asserts both his Hindu background and his triumphant universal humanism by denigrating the doctor's acquired Christianity and by quoting from all the cultural heritages he knows: Shakespeare, the Bible and the *Gita*. The incident somehow reveals himself to himself and leads to the writing of a second, more significant text:

> Waking in the night, he felt exposed and vulnerable . . . To do honour he had no gifts. He had no words to say what he wanted to say, the poet's words, which held more than

> the sum of their meanings. But awake one night . . . he got out of bed, . . . got paper and pencil and began to write. He addressed his mother. . . . He wrote of coming up to the brow of the hill, seeing the black, forked earth, the marks of the spade, the indentations of the fork prongs. He wrote of a journey he had made a long time before. He was tired; she made him rest. He was hungry; she gave him food. He had nowhere to go; she welcomed him (p. 484).

In this prose poem, the working of and belonging to the land, wandering, the mother, come together in a nurturing way; by exulting the mother, he achieves the "place" he yearns for. Mr Biswas reads his poem ("in prose") to the members of the literary group, exposing his entire soul in the process and getting drunk and sick. But, "the poem written, his self consciousness violated, he was whole again" (p. 484). Through his poem/narrative he has restored his mother's, his community's and his own honour. He has recognized, brought into the symbolic realm, a part of him which has hitherto been submerged; he has made a kind of peace with his past. And yet, the question arises: what kind of truth is achieved here? For in fact, the experience of welcome and nurturing exulted in the poem does not reflect the "reality" of the experience. At the time, Mr Biswas, returning misjudged and humiliated from his short trial as a pundit's apprentice, sought his mother's comfort and support and she had none to give him. Herself bereft, dislocated and dependent, she let him down, and it was in fact that experience which led, soon after, to Mr Biswas's final estrangement from his family and his embarking on his life of sign painting, etc. The narrator remarks at the time: ". . . nearly thirty years later, when he was a member of a small literary group in Port of Spain, he wrote and read out a simple poem in blank verse about the meeting. The disappointment, his surliness, all the unpleasantness was ignored, and the circumstances improved to allegory: the journey, the welcome, the food, the shelter" (p. 57).

In other words, to be incorporated into Mr Biswas's symbolic order, the past is idealized and allegorized. Its significance is not necessarily in its objective truth. The truth of memory is not the truth of fact. Language itself, a negation of presence, distorts, defers. However, to construct a self, what is needed, it seems, is a myth of the past, not the past itself. And for a brief moment, Mr Biswas achieves it.[26]

The moment, even as a moment of illusory wholeness, cannot stop Mr Biswas's decline, cannot win the battle against the void:

> Change had come over him without his knowing. There had been no precise point at which the city had lost its romance and promise, no point at which he had begun to consider himself old... He had grown to look upon houses as things that concerned other people.... They had ceased to rouse ambition or misery. He had lost the vision of the house. He sank into despair as into the void which, in his imagining, had always stood for the life he had yet to live (pp. 494–495).

The next and in many ways the last adventure in his picaresque wanderings, his stint as a community welfare officer (a position of supreme irony considering his own situation), seems like a step up but in fact, insofar as his life-in-language is concerned, constitutes a further step away from the expression of self. This job brings a sudden outward prosperity, including the acquisition of a car, but it also represents a greater inner withdrawal and an ever widening gap between reality and his inner life.

Mr Biswas's first duty in his new job is to conduct a survey of the area of which he is in charge and then to analyze the results. The sociological use of language attempts to interpret reality, to impose order and logic on it. It also brings Mr Biswas, for the first time in his life, in close touch with the seeming external forces that shape history: politics and social categories. Mr Biswas, however, is incapable of dealing with this kind of language: "And here he floundered.... He was dealing with a society that had no rules and patterns" (pp. 509–510). (This is, of course, also an implicit criticism of colonial practices of measuring one society by another's yardstick.) Although the report is eventually completed and copies are distributed in "various parts of the world," these words have no power to order the reality they deal with, and they are meaningless as far as Mr Biswas's relationship to language is concerned. If anything, they remove him a step further from himself. Indeed, the new job only emphasizes the horrors of reality:

> Life became nightmarish, divided between the tenement room and the area below the house. Shama continued to cook below the house. Sometimes the children slept there with the readers and learners; sometimes they slept with Mr Biswas in the tenement. And every afternoon, Mr Biswas drove to his area to spread knowledge of the finer things in life. He distributed booklets; he lectured; he formed organizations . . . (p. 529).

The final convergence of the disparate threads of Mr Biswas's life is the house on Sikkim Street. Needless to say, he is swindled once again—he pays three times what the house is worth, and it is so badly built that it is in imminent danger of collapsing (the dues Mr Biswas must pay for "place"). It continues to stand, however, and Mr Biswas even plants a garden. But this final stand proves to be only a final disintegration. Not having succeeded in finding a way to make life in the symbolic order encompass and define either reality or the past, Mr Biswas's decline and eventual death, his giving up of the forward-moving instinct, is almost inevitable. It is compounded by the departure of his two older children to study. Anand's departure is permanent (*his* killing of the father), and the legacy that he is bequeathed is the irrevocable split between life in the colonial symbolic order and origin.

Anand as Son and Father

In the last part of the novel the focalization shifts in large measure to Anand, his experiences at school, his relationship with his father, his observations of life around him. Anand, whose childhood and youth strongly resemble Naipaul's, is the eternal outsider, self-conscious, solitary, rawly sensitive. While clearly accepting the legacy of writing from his father (when Mrs Tulsi gives him a mixture of brandy and water to cure his chronic cough, he drinks it because it reminds him of Dickens), his emotional desertion of the family can only be explained as a repetition of the necessity to kill one's father in order to enter into the symbolic order of the alien written word. Anand's denial of his past, his severance from his history, allows him that entrance, but leaves him, just as it left Mr Biswas, a fragmented, dichotomized man, always searching for a way to be whole. At the same time, his identification with his father also involves incorporating his split.

Anand's prominence in the novel begins with Mr Biswas's attempt to "claim" him as he nears his breakdown at Green Vale. Although serving mainly as a way for Mr Biswas to ward off disintegration, Anand is initiated into his father's world of language: "He showed Anand how to mix colours. He taught him that red and yellow make orange, blue and yellow green" (p. 279). In other words, he teaches Anand the laws of combination and differentiation. He shares his scientific knowledge with him, and, most important, he moves with him into the unfinished house, the scene of his final breakdown. During the storm scene at the end of Part One, as Mr Biswas loses consciousness of the world around him, the focalization shifts to Anand. He descends with his father into the void: "He waited for his father to say something, to close the window, light the lamp. But Mr Biswas only muttered on the bed and the rain and wind swept through the room . . . Anand screamed and screamed" (p. 292). But he emerges from it with the help of others: "Anand saw a light swaying in the dark. It was a man . . . Ramkhilawan from the barracks" (p. 292). The light of his father's house goes out, the light of strangers comes to save him: "The oil lamp was not broken. There even remained some oil in it. The chimney was cracked, but still whole. Ramkhilawan brought out a damp box of matches from his trouser-pocket and put a lighted match to the wick. The wick, waterlogged, spluttered; the match burned down; the wick caught" (p. 293). Anand and Mr Biswas emerge into different lights. Mr Biswas's experience of the void gives him the strength (illusory as it is) to set out and inhabit the life in the word. For Anand it is the point of his own split. Abandoned by his father, being left to scream in the dark, Anand takes over the focalization (temporarily) and from about this time begins to nurse his own ambitions to become immersed in the proffered English culture and ultimately to escape his past.

As the first part of the novel is given its thematic impetus by the drowning of Mr Biswas's father, so the second part turns to a large extent on the incident of Anand's near drowning.

On a weekend of celebration mixed with nostalgia and sadness, Mrs Tulsi, her two sons and the Biswas family celebrate Owad's voyage to England for further studies. (Owad's journey to England is regarded enviously by Mr Biswas as yet another rung on the ladder of accession into the symbolic order of English culture, but one which he knows is closed to him.) The weekend spent with Owad sets in motion the drift of life to come. A repetition in reverse of the scene of the death of Mr Biswas's father by drowning, it marks Anand's entrance into the alien symbolic order and the beginning of Mr Biswas's decline. In the present scene, Anand is the one who is almost drowned, and Mr Biswas's life is not really in danger. Savi and Myna "burst into tears when they heard" (p. 356), as did Dehuti, Mr Biswas's sister, in the earlier scene. As a result of this episode Anand is put on a milk and prunes diet, a diet which supposedly provides the appropriate nourishment for a scholar, i.e., Mr Biswas decides that he should try and win an "exhibition." Anand's eventual success in the examination, followed by a scholarship to the local college and a scholarship for further study in England, leads to his permanent estrangement from Trinidad and his family, and more painfully, to his absence in the crucial period before Mr Biswas's death. During this period, from the drowning incident onwards, he leads a double life: the life of school, the inundation with English culture, and life at home where his relationship with his father is marked by painful identification alternating with increasing alienation and denial.

It is also significant that although Anand becomes a leading character in this part of the novel, and although the narration offers us glimpses of his thoughts and feelings, the motivation underlying the totality of his eventual desertion of his past remains a blank which can only really be understood as a symbolic repetition of the killing of the father and can only be filled out through an examination of Naipaul, the author's, later working through his past.

More specific to my discussion of language as holding the power of truth and the power of habitation is the immediate result of the near-drowning incident: "The next day Mr Biswas wrote an angry article about the lack of warning notices at Docksite" (p. 356). Anand, on the other hand, writes a composition in school about the incident in which for the first time he discards his teacher's directives and hints and writes directly about his experience:

> But in the last composition, there were no dashes and repetitions . . . only a walk to Docksite, a concrete sea-wall and liners in the distance. Mr Biswas read on, anxious to share the pain of the previous day. 'I raised my hand but I did not know if it got to the top. I opened my mouth to cry for help. Water filled it. I thought I was going to die and I closed my eyes because I did not want to look at the water' (p. 357).

For Anand, this near death brings about a true rebirth—into the power of language. Anand (and Naipaul by inference), it would seem, can find a way to ground his reality authentically in language. However, at the same time, the other aspect of his legacy from his father undermines the possibility of creating a complete self in language: the split from and denial of the past which is made clear at the end of the novel. For Mr Biswas, reading Anand's composition, comparing it to his own expression in writing (the angry article) which is nothing more than a cover up of his real pain and fear, is a recognition of his own failure to make the written word the instrument of truth and the death of his ambition—a killing of the father. This ritual "killing" is given its final stamp in the joke Anand plays on Mr Biswas: ". . . that evening, just before Mr Biswas sat at the table, Anand pulled the chair from under him, and Mr Biswas fell noisily to the floor" (p. 358).

The authentic written expression of experience rendered in this scene by Anand is highlighted through yet another contrast. The phrases that Anand's teacher suggests for Anand's composition are drawn from stereotypical English holiday situations: "project a visit—feverish preparations—eager anticipation—laden hampers—. . . spirits overflowing into song—. . . energetically battling the waves—cries of delirious joy . . . " (p. 356). Anand rejects those phrases in favour of his own stark narrative. But months later, when Mr Biswas, a civil servant, is offered the use of a house by the sea, the family's experience there is described in words very similar to the ones supplied by Anand's teacher for the writing of his composition. For then Mr Biswas's life has acquired a veneer which seems to correspond most closely with his adopted culture, although its substance is no more real than those hackneyed phrases.

Corresponding to Mr Biswas's losing battle with unification is Anand's progress through the symbolic order and concomitant ambivalent relationship with his father. He too discovers the power of the word to foreshadow reality in unexpected ways. Showing off one afternoon to Hari (a pundit brother-in-law) and his wife, he recites a poem: "Bingen On the Rhine" (Mr Biswas's favourite poem of long ago), beginning "A soldier lay dying in Algiers." Encouraged by what seems to be the influence of his recitation on his audience, he declaims the last stanza with increasing pathos: "'Tell her the last night of my life, for ere the moon be risen,/ My body will be out of pain, my soul be out of prison.'" Hari's wife begins weeping. "Less than a week later, Hari died. It was only then that Anand learned that Hari had known for some time that he was going to die soon" (p. 415).

As Anand becomes more and more immersed in school life he becomes increasingly aware of his father's inadequacies and humiliations. One attempt to communicate with his father takes the form of storytelling:

> One evening, after a quarrel had flared up and died down [between Mr Biswas and Shama] without being concluded, Anand went to Mr Biswas's room and said. 'I have a story to tell you . . . Once upon a time there was a man—' Anand's voice broke. 'Yes?' Mr Biswas said, in a mocking friendly voice, still smiling, scraping his lower lip with his teeth. 'Once upon a time there was a man who—' His voice broke again, his father's smile confused him, he forgot what he had planned to say and abandoning grammar, added quickly, 'Who, whatever you do for him, wasn't satisfied.' Mr Biswas burst out laughing, and Anand ran out of the room, trembling with rage and

> humiliation, to the kitchen, where Shama comforted him (pp. 378–379).

At the end of the book, in an oblique reference to Anand/Naipaul as the future writer, the narrator comments on the house at Sikkim Street:

> Soon it seemed to the children that they had never lived anywhere but in the tall square house in Sikkim Street. From now their lives would be ordered, their memories coherent. The mind, while it is sound, is merciful. And rapidly the memories of Hanuman House, The Chase, Green Vale, Shorthills, the Tulsi house in Port of Spain would become jumbled, blurred; events would be telescoped, many forgotten. Occasionally a nerve of memory would be touched—a puddle reflecting the blue sky after rain, a pack of thumbed cards, the fumbling with a shoelace . . . and a fragment of forgotten experience would be dislodged, isolated, puzzling. In a northern land, in a time of new separations and yearnings, in a library grown suddenly dark, the hailstones beating against the windows, the marbled endpaper of a dusty leatherbound book would disturb: and it would be the hot noisy week before Christmas in the Tulsi Store: the marbled patterns of oldfashioned balloons powdered with a rubbery dust in a shallow white box that was not to be touched. So later, and very slowly, in securer times of different stresses, when the memories had lost the power to hurt, with pain or joy, they would fall into place and give back the past (p. 581).

For Naipaul at this stage of his writing career, then, the only possible autobiographical act was to use the borrowed form of the novel to recreate imaginatively the sources of his lack of self and a past. And yet the past, as given back in the novel, does not make him whole. The emptiness, the void at the core continues to haunt his writing and determine his life. In the novel, Anand is, somehow, finally missing. The novel itself, the inhabitation of the word for Naipaul, can only perpetuate the split while tracing it.

CHAPTER TWO

The Overcrowded Barracoon

The Overcrowded Barracoon,[1] a collection of articles written over a period of fourteen years and published in 1972, belongs to the corpus of the non-fiction of Naipaul's middle period. The earliest article, "London," was written in 1958, during Naipaul's early years as a fiction writer in London, a period whose high point was the publication of *A House for Mr Biswas* in 1960, and the latest, the title article, was published in 1972, closing a decade and a half of extensive travel which yielded a rich crop of works: non-fictional (travel and history) and fictional (novels and short stories).

As a collection of essays spanning a considerable part of Naipaul's writing career, *The Overcrowded Barracoon* develops most of the themes and displays many of the attitudes reflected in the longer non-fiction writing of his middle period.[2] I have thus chosen it as a representative example of the manifestation of the cultural displacement and quest for origin in Naipaul's life-as-writer at this time, and of the preoccupations which constituted his turning away from fiction.[3] A second reason for choosing this work for analysis is the way it highlights the blurring of genre boundaries in current theories of autobiography.

In the course of this period, Naipaul's autobiographical purpose, in particular his quest for origin (at this stage undifferentiated from the idea of a myth of origin), was transposed onto intellectual objectives, but the underlying pressure it continued to exert resulted in works, such as *The Overcrowded Barracoon*, which can be seen both as steps in the evolution towards a "true" autobiography, and as "marginal" autobiographies in their own right. On the one hand *The Overcrowded Barracoon* fulfills the basic "rules" of autobiography set down by one of the outstanding theorists of autobiography, Elizabeth Bruss,[4] on the other it stretches those rules to a point where we must ask ourselves whether autobiography can be contained within any formal description, or whether the autobiographical impulse, which exists in every text, can or should be "made" into a genre. The way this book destabilizes the definition of autobiography, by existing as it were on its very boundaries, can be seen as a formal translation of Naipaul's need to find a way outside of traditional conventions to reconstitute his self.

The Quest for Origin

As a collection of articles written over a period of fourteen years, *The Overcrowded Barracoon* testifies to Naipaul's peripatetic career as a travelling writer/journalist. This period followed the early stage of his writing life in which he attempted to fulfill his original ambition, formed as part of his ascendance into the symbolic order of the word, to be a writer of fiction in the tradition of the nineteenth-century English novel. The earlier phase reached its peak in the writing of *A House for Mr Biswas*, followed by the less successful *Mr Stone and the Knights Companion*,[5] but culminated in a sense of frustration, occasioned by his essential split, both with fiction as a vehicle and with his position as outsider in England. One might say that in the following two decades Naipaul attempted to work against the split by: a) attempting to ground existence in a rich, external writing experience—life in the word; and b) displacing the personal problem of split self and lack of a myth of origin onto an intellectual exploration of the relationship between colonialism and post-colonialism, myth-making and history.[6] Part of that project also involved, in *The Loss of El Dorado*, for example, an attempt to find his personal history through an imaginative linking up with the forgotten factual history of Trinidad. But at the same time, the split continued its work in him. In the first place, his career as journalist and traveller uncannily repeated the story of his father's ultimately unfulfilling career as journalist and his search for house/place as portrayed in the figure of Mr Biswas. In the second place, the underlying themes and structures of *The Overcrowded Barracoon* express the continued enactment of the split and loss of myth of origin through the signifying chain.

Form and theme meet, in *The Overcrowded Barracoon,* in a seemingly contradictory process. While the narrating "I" is gradually absented from the text (from the position of subject in the first articles to a detached observer in the last), reflecting the repression of the autobiographical impetus, the intellectual, non-fiction project which "takes over" and dominates the writing traces a shift from a quest for lost origin to a recognition of origin as myth, a construct, and consequently to the possibility that the solution to the writing of autobiography lies in the writer as myth-maker. The integration of the "I" through the conscious creation of a myth of origin and of an appropriate formal mode, however, will succeed only later, in the third phase of writing.

I.

The first four essays comprising the section called "An Unlikely Colonial" establish Naipaul the narrator as the split, or rather incomplete, self and introduce the themes of the entire middle period. These themes all derive from the central issue in Naipaul's writing, the relation of language to experience and the self, which in turn arises from the subject split between the symbolic order of the alien word and the lost past—origin and its substitute myth of origin. Can the written word of an alien tongue serve as a means to recover the past of another culture? Or are all attempts to recover origin essentially myth-making, and how does that affect one who is denied a myth of origin, or who adopts a myth of non-origin?

The myth of non-origin finds its most coherent expression in the first section of the book in the motif of naming. It is not accidental that the titles of the first four essays are names: the name of a place, a game, a flower, a segment of a people. All are names which represent a code, an aspect of Western/English culture, and all are, as far as the narrator is concerned, the wrong name. Or to be more precise, they exhibit the gap between name and named which constitutes Naipaul's experience of the Name-of-the-usurper-Father. Three aspects of naming as part of the ascendance into the symbolic order of the word are evoked here: the names of codes of the alien culture—cricket and literature; the name of the subject coming into being —East Indian; and the name of origin/place. In all cases the names taken on or received obliterate and thus nullify the nameless past.

Language thus comes to substitute for origin and experience. "Cricket" and "Jasmine" relate to two major components of the alien cultural code: morals and social values and literature/language. Both are components of the colonial education but they remain unintegrated. The British public school code represented by cricket provided Trinidad with "skill, courage, style: the graces. . . ." (p. 20). Trinidad, as Naipaul experienced it, was a vacuum filled by British imperialism: "To dismiss it would be . . . to fail to see that these territories are a unique imperial creation. . . . To be a nationalist . . . you must have a nation. . . . The West Indian, whatever his community, had only this 'system'" (p. 21). To this must be added the observation that Trinidad was made up primarily of a community of cultural transplants whose links with their original culture were already severed in terms of place.[7]

If cricket names a system of values and a code of behaviour, English literature, in "Jasmine," "was like an alien mythology. . . . To us, without a mythology, all literatures were foreign" (p. 24). But the burden of literature, of language, is even greater: "If landscapes do not start to be real until they have been interpreted by an artist, so, until they have been written about, societies appear to be without shape and *embarrassing*" (p. 26). Language, then, in a true post-structuralist sense, creates experience. Furthermore, "fiction or any work of the imagination . . . hallows its subject" (p. 26), i.e., creates mythologies which give us a past. The symbols of English literature evoked only ungrounded fantasy. The physical sensory experiences of childhood remained unnamed. And even though in later years Naipaul found the courage in his own words, "to give a quality of myth to what was agreed to be petty and ridiculous—Frederick Street in Port of Spain, Marine Square, the districts of Laventille and Barataria" (p. 26), i.e., to become a myth-maker himself, he had not succeeded, when this essay was written, in closing the gap between the named and unnamed: "Jasmine, jasmine. But the word and the flower had been separate in my mind for too long. They did not come together" (p. 31).

To name the unnamed or the unnameable—this notion extends in more than one direction. As a fiction writer, Naipaul found the courage to name the physical surroundings of his childhood and use them as material for his early novels. But the confrontation with the past, the recognition and acceptance of his severance from a myth of origin (rather than the denial of its existence), was still at this point unaccomplished. In "Jasmine" he relates that the starting point that allowed him to begin writing authentically about Trinidad was provided by some "local short stories . . . never published outside Trinidad" (p. 27). These stories provided him with a tradition of writing, however minimal. The author of these stories is unnamed, but most scholars agree that it was probably his father, Seepersad Naipaul. It would take Naipaul almost twenty years more to "name" his father and his role in his loss of a myth of origin.[8]

To name oneself within the language of an alien culture is a problem which extends to the writing of autobiography itself. Naipaul's struggle with the genre thus may be seen as a problem of naming himself within an alien code of language and thought. How can the non-Western part of himself, the lost past, be integrated in a Western construct? One way this conflict is externalized in *The Overcrowded Barracoon* is in the preoccupation with other people's autobiographies, especially those which bring to the fore the existence between two worlds.

The second article, "Cricket," is one such example. It serves Naipaul as a borrowed text, and a borrowed autobiography at that. The experience described in it is similar to his own, as he himself admits, but it is at one remove: Naipaul is absolved from "naming" his own past directly. Our path to Naipaul's childhood is filtered through a body of writing which is itself an interpretation of another's experience: the adoption of the alien culture by the colonial child. In the case of C. L. R. James, the symbol of the received culture is the code of cricket (the other, derived meaning of the word, denoting "the right way to behave," adds a retrospective irony to the article). At one point in the narration C. L. R. James and Naipaul merge not only in content but in narrative voice: "But we have ended up speaking the same language; and though England is not perhaps the country we thought it was, we have both charmed ourselves away from Trinidad. *'For the inner self'*, as Mr James writes, *'the die was cast'*" (p. 23, my italics). The pun on the word "die" is also, perhaps, not accidental.

Nevertheless, James's autobiography is an appropriated text and the act of borrowing makes Naipaul a usurper, which suggests his profound internalization of the colonizing usurper father's code, and thus in another way repeats his entrapment within Western concepts of history and writing.

Learning to name within a given code is one side of a coin the other of which is to be named as a subject within a cultural context. In "East Indian" the Trinidadian East Indian is suspended between two existences. While Indian rituals survive in the new world, "India is no more than the memory of a depressed rural existence that survived in Trinidad until only the other day" (p. 38). But in the adopted motherland, England, to be a Trinidadian Indian is not only to be a colonial, but an "unlikely" one at that: "To be an Indian or East Indian from the West Indies is to be a perpetual surprise to people outside the region" (p. 35). "To be an Indian from Trinidad . . . is, in addition to everything else, to be the embodiment of an old verbal ambiguity" (p. 36). The name "Indian" which signifies Naipaul's origin is deprived of meaning by the appropriations of Columbus and his colonizing followers. Whether he is an East Indian, or a West Indian East Indian, or an East Indian West Indian or British Indian, according to whoever is naming him, all the names have meaning only within the context of colonialism and create an unstable relationship between the name and its meaning which extends to the name and its bearer. Naipaul's collective name has been usurped by the colonizing system of language and is thus a substitute. He has no definition other than this colonial appellation—his origin is lost.

The sequence of articles in "An Unlikely Colonial" is presented so that it begins with place, the "wrong" place—London, and ends with a triple image of travel which traces the entire cycle of Naipaul's quest for origin at this time. In the first,

Naipaul is suspended between two cultures on a flight between London and Paris; in the second, the mass immigration of Indians to Trinidad is evoked; in the third, to come full cycle, Hindus in Trinidad enact through ritual the return to the homeland and the faith:

> The holy city of Benares is far away but the young Hindu at his initiation ceremony in Port of Spain will still take up his staff and beggar's bowl and say that he is off to Benares to study. His relatives will plead with him, and in the end he will lay down his staff, and there will be a ritual expression of relief (p. 38).

"London" is a place which embodies Naipaul's myth of non-origin, fixing a point of departure for *The Overcrowded Barracoon* in general and for the emergence of the itinerant writer. London is the place in which Naipaul writes but "it is not a place I can write about" (p. 16). Thus "An Unlikely Colonial" marks the parameters of the period, from the wrong place to wandering. The voyaging, as a quest, signaled in "East Indian," is both the excuse for and the metaphoric vehicle of the "India" section.

II.

If "An Unlikely Colonial" maps the incompleteness of the writer in the life in the word through lack of origin, "India" is both the quest for myth of origin, beginnings, and the embodiment of its frustration.

Autobiography is, as I have claimed, contingent on having a cultural myth of origin, the making of the subject. India, as the origin of Naipaul's forebears, besides being a fitting subject for his emerging views on the Third World and ex-colonial societies in particular, thus drew Naipaul as a possible source (Naipaul's grandfather was one of the indentured labourers brought to Trinidad in the nineteenth century to overcome labour shortages in the British colony). However, the conflict created between this quest and the need to repudiate the past colours, even dominates his response to India.[9] In *The Overcrowded Barracoon*, India, rather than projecting an image of completeness, is in itself a metaphoric replaying of the split subject, an additional signifier in the chain of Naipaul's life in the word. Not only does it not yield his beginnings but it remains impenetrable and unnameable, demonstrating through this repetition how locked Naipaul is in his split.

This dual object/subject function, which recalls, perhaps, the transition in the ascendance into the symbolic order,[10] indicates the two levels which I would like to consider here. "India" is read in two ways simultaneously: as a collection of articles depicting aspects of India's complexity and contradictions, and as Naipaul/the narrator's encounter with India, and its significance for him. Both readings yield the irrecoverability of origin.

Naipaul's engagement with India as represented in *The Overcrowded Barracoon* is fixed at a single crucial episode in India's history—its encounter with the West via British imperialism—and hence is experienced as a conflict between constituting a source, origin, and being a colony subjugated, usurped, deprived of history. Of all his writings on India, Naipaul chose for *The Overcrowded Barracoon* those essays that are constituted as a repetition of his own existence as a split subject: He is writing, inhabiting the word of the alien father, bringing his Western modes of thought and language to his subject matter, and at the same time is on an unceasing quest for origin.

The "India" section is also transitional in terms of the narrating "I." While in "In the Middle of the Journey" the narrating "I" is still the subject, in the other articles the narrator becomes an observer, albeit emotionally involved in what he sees. Just as the quest for origin is doomed to fail in terms of "India as history," because Naipaul can only apprehend it at a point of conflict between East and West, so at the level of narration the "I" is gradually overtaken by the described external content. Far from being a solution to the problem of origin India is thus a trigger for the tenuous self to disappear.

"In the Middle of the Journey" explicitly establishes these two parallel processes. In reference to India as origin, Naipaul says:

> A colonial, in the double sense of one who had grown up in a Crown colony and one who had been cut off from the metropolis, be it either England or India, I came to India expecting to find metropolitan attitudes. . . . And I have been surprised by similarities. In India, as in tiny Trinidad, I have found the feeling that the metropolis is elsewhere, in Europe or America (p. 48).

In other words, India, too, is a split subject, its origin/place/ metropolis usurped, repressed, displaced. In India, Naipaul does not find "place" but only the sense of displacement: India's encounter with colonialism has wiped out its origin. Origin is always elsewhere, for Naipaul and for India, his origin.

On the other hand, Naipaul is conscious of his voyage through India as a losing of the "I": ". . . I have never before been in streets where everyone is Indian, where I blend unremarkably into the crowd. This has been curiously deflating, for all my life I have expected some recognition of my difference. . . . To be one of four hundred and thirty-nine million Indians is terrifying" (p. 48). To sink into origin is then to sink into oblivion, void, non-differentiation, whereas self exists only in a differing relation to other. For Naipaul, however, the prospect of oneness is not a homecoming. The solution to the lack of origin must ultimately be found within the symbolic order, as an aspect of the split subject. When the fantasy of the past becomes a realization it turns out to be a regressive fantasy.

The ferociousness and bitterness of the response of the narrating "I" to the India it experiences throughout the essays betrays an involvement far greater than that of a mere "travelling writer." Fundamentally, India is experienced as a void filled with unnameable objects:

> Perhaps India is only a word, a mystical idea that embraces all those vast plains and rivers through which the train moves, all those anonymous figures asleep on railway platforms and the footpaths of Bombay, all those poor fields and stunted animals, all this exhausted plundered land. Perhaps it is this, this vastness which no one can ever get to know: India as an ache, for which one has a great tenderness, but from which at length one always wishes to separate oneself (pp. 50–51).

India as void is peopled with the symbols of Naipaul's own conflict: place (plundered land), quest (rivers, railway platforms) and namelessness (anonymous figures), carried to a huge, non-differentiated oneness: "all" those vast plains, "all" those anonymous figures, etc. At the same time this passage illustrates the shift from the "I" as subject to absent subject. "India as an ache, which *no one* can ever get to know; India as an ache for which *one* has a great tenderness, but . . . *one* always wishes to separate *oneself*" (my italics). The use of "one" here has a double effect: First, it distances the narrator from the events, detaches him. But it is also a shift from the individual to the collective, the universal. Thus while attempting to distance himself from India, Naipaul is also at the same time sinking into "all that vastness." Furthermore, India as origin, Naipaul is saying, cannot be known by a "one." To be a "one," one must separate "oneself" from origin.

The perception of India as a devouring void alternates with descriptions of India as void filled up, impenetrable: "Because it is the simplicity of India which disappoints and in the end fatigues. . . . India lies all on the surface" (p. 87). Or: "The palace rose out of this dust; it expressed this dust, nothing more; it is returning to dust again. . . . There is no tragedy" (p. 84). The spatial vastness is matched by time unrecoverable: "The infinite, metaphysical timelessness: it always came to this" (p. 86).

Naipaul applies his Western-bred intellect and its sense of the past and history to India, his origin, and finds it unfathomable. This failure is projected onto India's so-called failure to come to grips with its own past: " . . . the Indian intellectual failure, which is less a failure of the individual intellect than the deficiency of a closed civilization, ruled by ritual and myth" (p. 94). Naipaul's frustration gives way to irrational, hyperbolic generalizations which often resemble the exaggerations and absurdities which he sees in India's engagement with the West: "India possesses only its unexamined past and its pathetic spirituality" (p. 105); "A nation ceaselessly exchanging banalities with itself" (p. 95).

And, finally, India is his own predicament: "Every discipline, skill and proclaimed ideal of the modern Indian state is a copy of something which is known to exist in its true form somewhere else" (p. 102); "Local judgement is valueless. It is even as if, without the foreign chit, Indians can have no confirmation of their own reality" (p. 103).

To focus more specifically on the way Naipaul's experience of India in the quest for origin constitutes yet another signifier of his own condition I will briefly discuss two related essays: "Autobiography of an Unknown Indian" and "The Last of the Aryans" which are, not accidentally, presented consecutively in the section.

Both essays focus on books written by Nirad Chaudhuri, one his own autobiography as an individual, the other, a collective autobiography, on the origins of India. In "Autobiography of an Unknown Indian" Naipaul singles out Chaudhuri's autobiography from among four other Indian autobiographies, all of which, again, are evaluated in terms of their relation to the East-West encounter. Whereas Chaudhuri is praised for his conscious problematization of that encounter, the other four are belittled for being oblivious to the problem, thus betraying their being of the East and unequipped for writing autobiographies.[11] Interestingly, however, in order to examine the problematic relation between autobiography and experience in each case, Naipaul chooses signifiers which dominate his own experience: place and language, and, moreover, he locates them so that they begin and end the essay, thus framing it.

In the first instance, in the first paragraph of the essay, Naipaul claims that for Ghandi, one of the autobiographers under discussion, "A place is its name." While using this phrase to condemn Ghandi for being oblivious to cultural differences, Naipaul is in fact inadvertently granting Ghandi what he himself is in quest of and cannot achieve—the bridging of the gap between symbolic order and origin, signifier and signified. In contrast, Naipaul ends the article with the breakdown of the symbolic order: the inability of the English language to convey Indian experience. He quotes from Tanden, another of the autobiographers, who is, of course, unconscious of the problem: "Gradually a new picture began to build in our minds, of India coming out of the Kal Yug into a new era of freedom and plenty, Ram Rajya." Naipaul comments: "Language has at last broken down. Gao Mata, Ram Rajya: for these there are no English equivalents . . . . In the definition of Ram Rajya the true stress falls on 'plenty,' while 'freedom' is an intrusive English *word*. Here is the futility of the Indo-English encounter" (pp. 65–66).

It is not only these autobiographers' lack of self-consciousness which disturbs Naipaul, however, but the effects of the transposition of one cultural experience onto another: " . . . and in [Indian] autobiographies the lack of wonder is frequently converted into a hectic self-love" (p. 61). Or later: "And it is in this bastard form—in which a religious view of life, laudable in one culture, is converted steadily into self-love, disagreeable in another culture—that we can begin to see the misunderstandings and futility of the Indo-English encounter" (p. 63).

From his ambivalent standpoint of identifying with the difficulties of Indian autobiographers on the one hand and judging them from within his adopted intellectual framework on the other, Naipaul opts to praise "The Autobiography of an Unknown Indian," which problematizes precisely that duality. In the context of *The Overcrowded Barracoon*, the "unknown" of the title is heavily overdetermined. Besides suggesting a deviation in the tradition of autobiography by recording the life of an unknown, a non-celebrity, the word "unknown" echoes and reverses the "no one" of "In the Middle of the Journey": unknown as non-subject, unknown to himself, or even one of a kind.

"The Last of the Aryans," the following article, is important not only as a complement to the former, but in that it is preoccupied with the paradoxical relation between having and being origin, a question which informs the entire second half of *The Overcrowded Barracoon* and which is the crux of a possible resolution to Naipaul's autobiographical impetus.

"The Last of the Aryans" focuses on a second book by Chaudhuri, *The Continent of Circe* (the title once again evokes Naipaul's own experience of India), which attempts to trace India's collective origins, and by inference deals with the connection between the discovery of new worlds, the problem of origin and the split subject.

The Aryans who settled in the Gangetic Plain embody the paradox of origin. As creators of a new civilization, they were beginners, and for Naipaul ancestors, origin. But as originators seeking wholeness in an empty world they were bedeviled by two problems. The first was the issue of their own origin, the quest for which cannot be eradicated: "The snow-capped Himalayas have become objects of pilgrimage; and some Hindus, in their hysteria, look beyond that to the North Pole. . . There, someone will tell you in all the blaze of Madras, there at the North Pole lies the true home of the Hindus" (p. 74). Origin, then, is always elsewhere. The second issue is the other. As all seekers of pristine worlds of wholeness discover, there are always others, usually "natives" to be reckoned with, subjugated or even exterminated. In the case of the Aryans, the Darks, the indigenous Australoids, were kept in strict segregation and subjugation but nevertheless posed a threat to the Aryans' sense of wholeness and continuity. This is evident in the Hindu myth told by Chaudhuri and retold by Naipaul. A Dark, performing Aryan religious rites, causes the death of the son of a Brahmin, and is decapitated as a punishment by Rana, the Aryan hero. The Brahmin's son is consequently revived. To be originators, then, otherness must be denied, excluded.

III.

The role of this otherness in relation to self and myth of origin is explored in greater depth in "Columbus and Crusoe," the title essay of the final section of *The Overcrowded Barracoon*.

"Columbus and Crusoe" deals with two originators, historical and fictional: Christopher Columbus and Robinson Crusoe. Both constitute the conflict between being and having origin. Columbus, in reality a cruel, mean-spirited and banal man, has engendered an enduring myth of the heroic, almost divine conquest of the new world, and hence has become a double originator: as the prototypic, founding ancestor of Central and Latin American Spanish people, and as the embodiment of the myth of the discoverer. Columbus, however, had to contend with history and reality: his new world was peopled with others, his expeditions dictated by circumstances. Crusoe, on the other hand, is the fictional true originator, the man in an empty world who endures the terrors of discovery only to relinquish that position and return to "civilization," the slave society of Brazil.

The dream of a new world, of discovering an empty world is at one and the same time a dream of total power, of being an originator, a myth-maker, and a dream of origin, of an undifferentiated world, a world without other. "The dream of the untouched, complete world, the thing for ourselves alone, the dream of Shangri-la, is an enduring human fantasy" (p. 224). Herein lies the paradox of the subject. Selfhood is contingent on the existence of other, whether as an imaginary, internalized idealized self, or as Other, the Law of the Father, a key to entering the symbolic order. The quest for wholeness, origin, is the quest of the split subject, coming from within the symbolic order and hence always doomed to be frustrated, just as Naipaul's quest for origin outside the Western construct of the symbolic order cannot be fulfilled. On the other hand, being origin, a myth-maker, or, as in the case of Defoe, a writer, opens up the possibility of perhaps constructing a myth of origin, presupposing beginning.

Columbus, then, like the Aryans, is the prototypic historical split subject who engenders a myth of origin. Crusoe, on the other hand, is a fictional hero granted the fulfillment of the fantasy: the desert island, solitude, the empty world, "the dream of total power" (p. 225). But, as Naipaul writes, for the discoverer, "The discovery . . . could not but be horrible"—in the case of Columbus the necessity of subduing or exterminating the other as the price of wholeness which leads to non-self, in the case of Crusoe, the terror of being an originator, paradoxically both being origin and lacking origin.

O. Mannoni[12] sees Crusoe as a man working through a regressive "misanthropic neurosis" on the desert island, driven by a neurotic need for solitude, slowly regaining health by learning to live with "other," and eventually returning to society. The desert island metaphor can be further extended to include not just a neurosis but an existential condition of the split subject: the quest for a desert island as a quest for origin, wholeness, non-differentiation, and the gradual coming into subjectivity through the recognition of otherness. Crusoe is the fulfillment of the "dream of being the first man in the world, of watching the first crop grow. . . . it is the dream . . . of possessing 'the first gun that had been fired there since the creation of the world'. It is the dream of total power" (pp. 224–225). As the ejection image implies, this is the dream of being not the only man but the first procreator. This state of oneness, however, precludes other and thus self as subject in the symbolic order. As soon as Friday and others come onto the scene a problem arises: "Where do sanctions start in the empty world?" (p. 225). How to reconcile giving sanctions, i.e., being an originator, with recognizing other, i.e., being a subject who is inserted into a continuing chain of history?

Thus far the discussion has been about the myth-maker, the colonizer. What of the colonized, the subjugated "Dark" and his role in the question of self and origin?

Mannoni sees the native as an object upon which the colonizer projects his repressed desires: incest, aggression, etc.[13] From Naipaul's discussion, too, the native emerges as an object, a non-subject. Naipaul quotes Crusoe: "I likewise taught him to say master, and then let him know that was to be my name" (p. 225). Here again is another variant on naming: for the native, name and function have been collapsed into one signifier. His ascendance into language and his most basic instrument of communication within that language, are contingent on a position of inferiority and dependence which erases his own otherness. It is not that a native has no need for origin, it is that as he is not granted autonomous otherness by the colonizer, as he is not a subject, he does not acquire a myth of origin. Perceived through a Western subject, he remains an object. Thus, by extension, Naipaul, writing from within the Western symbolic order, despite his intellectual condemnation of colonialism, cannot grant the "native" part of himself the status of subject and is hence deprived of a myth of origin. He is trapped within his Western constructs.[14]

IV.

The themes of "Columbus and Crusoe," the split between having and being origin, myth-making vs. "Dark," are reflected in the structural arrangement of the final two sections of *The Overcrowded Barracoon*. In fact, by opening the final section, and thus being positioned midway between the two sections "Columbus and Crusoe" "presides" over the split subject.

At the beginning of this chapter I stated that *The Overcrowded Barracoon* traces the gradual absenting of the split "I" as subject/narrator, while displacing and taking up the predicament and quest of that "I" in the actual material of the essays. This process reaches its culmination in the second half of the book which has two sections: "Looking Westward" and "Columbus and Crusoe." First, the involved observer of the "India" section is transformed into a more or less detached onlooker, often described in the third person as "the visiting writer" or simply "the visitor." Second, one group contains articles on four figures, the other on six societies. The four figures of "Looking Westward" (the title is telling) are all individuals, writers and myth-makers, while the subjects of the articles in "Columbus and Crusoe" are post-colonial, former slave societies lacking history and deprived of a myth of origin. In the second half of *The Overcrowded Barracoon* Naipaul thus employs a spatial metaphor for his inner state of being.

But while *The Overcrowded Barracoon* clearly reflects Naipaul's inner structure in this period—recognition of lack, quest for origin, registering of split—it also contains the seed of the future resolution and its expression in genre. The crux of this resolution lies in the relationship between history and myth, fiction and non-fiction, as articulated in "Columbus and Crusoe." The recognition of the role of myth in history, and of the idea that selfhood requires not origin itself but, in relinquishing it, some kind of fictionalizing of it, opens up the possibility for the writer, the myth-maker, to invent his own myth of origin.

Another example of this direction is the writing of *The Loss of El Dorado* (1969), Naipaul's attempt to create a personal history out of the imaginative and dramatic rewriting of the history of Trinidad, and specifically of the region of his birth and childhood, on the basis of forgotten historical documents. This work, says Peter Hughes, gave Naipaul "a second historical relation with his origin that coexisted with the fictive relation created by his novels."[15] To my mind, like the fiction of the middle period and like *The Overcrowded Barracoon* itself, *The Loss of El Dorado* is an expression of Naipaul's conflict. It does indeed foreshadow the creation of personal history, or myth of origin through writing and through an imaginative, not to say fictive, casting of historical facts. On the other hand, it is a displacement of the personal lack, what Naipaul himself called "my own sense of being cut off from a past,"[16] onto a collective lack and an intellectual solution, thereby continuing to evade the confrontation with the personally felt void. Not accidentally, perhaps, this history concerns the Indian Chaguanes (the name of Naipaul's birthplace) who were obliterated by imperialist conquests, of whom Naipaul writes in the Foreword: "The disappearance is unimportant; *it is part of nobody's story*" (p. 14, my italics). At this stage Naipaul is still, to himself, nobody. Only later, with the writing of *Finding the Centre* and finally *The Enigma of Arrival*, can Naipaul become somebody first by confronting his own void and his complete severance from his past, and then by constructing a myth of origin as a new beginning.

V.

The second half of *The Overcrowded Barracoon*, as already noted, registers the split between the Western myth-maker, originator and non-origin, the "Dark." And indeed a closer reading reveals that each section can be read as a single unit, its articles as variations on a theme.

In "Looking Westward" the four essays revolve around four bodies of written texts in different spheres, the relation of those texts to the reality they purport to engage with, and the powers and responsibilities of the originators of the texts, the writers, to find history or to create it. The overall question which seems to emerge from "Looking Westward" echoes the themes of *A House for Mr Biswas* —the struggle between being shaped by the word and using the word to create history or myth. The stance taken towards this question in "Looking Westward" is ambivalent. While each of the figures is acknowledged and even celebrated as a figure of power as a writer, together they are ultimately seen as failed visionaries whose texts are either ineffective or out of their control. In the section "Columbus and Crusoe," on the other hand, text is diffuse and of the present, recording those societies' struggle with the lack of past, origin, continuity, the legacy of colonialism and slavery.

The four types of texts which constitute the axes of the four articles of "Looking Westward"—visionary writing in "Mr Matsuda's Million-Dollar Gamble," fiction writing in "Steinbeck in Monterey," political writing in "New York with Norman Mailer" and anthropological/sociological writing in "Jacques Soustelle and the Decline of the West,"—represent the main modes of written texts known in the West. In addition, numerous other kinds of texts abound: advertisements, extra-textual summaries, interviews and, of course, Naipaul's text itself which incorporates them all, thus situating itself in their history.

Myths can be engendered unawares, as in the case of Steinbeck and *Cannery Row*, and defeat even the writer's intentions and philosophy: "To be received into fairyland; it is a strange fate for Steinbeck, the novelist of social conscience, the angry man of the 1930s . . . the man who always scoffed at the myth-making capacities of his Peninsula" (p. 176). Steinbeck's text has a perverse dynamics. On the one hand it has engendered a reality which is a travesty of its vision; on the other, it is itself a mythologized rendering of reality: "'He hurt California terribly. . . . I've no background of being able to say this book's better than that one, but it hurt me to read *The Grapes*. It wasn't factual enough. You know what an Okie is?'" (p. 182).

Mailer, on the other hand, "had told a television reporter that running a campaign was like writing a novel. . . . 'When a writer finishes a novel he is a changed man'" (p. 187). "From press reports it appeared that Mailer was attempting a re-make of *Armies*. A false start—this was admitted later—but a writer's false start: the new book often begins like a repeat of the one just finished" (p. 186). Mailer, of whom Naipaul is gently ironic, and Mr Matsuda, who is patently absurd, both try to impose their corrective myth of the past on reality, Matsuda through an unfocused, distorted view of the West, Mailer through a vision engendered by his self-image as a writer: "It was as though, during the campaign, Mailer had redefined his writer's role by negatives. He couldn't assess the value of the campaign. 'If you don't win, you change very little'" (pp. 204–205).

In the article on Jacques Soustelle we find an aspect of Naipaul himself. A child who never knew his real father, Soustelle is nurtured by a series of "very good men"—his stepfather, and a teacher "who helped and guided and arranged the scholarship examinations which led to Paris and the Ecole Normale Superieure when he was seventeen . . . 'By the time I was twenty I had sat twelve competitive examinations'" (p. 211). Soustelle "appears to be two men" (p. 206), scholar and politician. He embarked on his own quest for origin in his researches of the Otomi tribe of Mexico and the Aztec civilization. The Aztec universe was destroyed by the Spanish, but Soustelle takes an ambivalent stance between colonizer and colonized: "'The Spaniards couldn't have acted otherwise. And we mustn't forget the efforts some Spaniards made to record and defend; or that they made possible the society in which Indian life was to reawaken'" (pp. 212–213).

Soustelle's scholarship, his text, which is a repetition of those Spanish attempts to "record and defend," engenders the myth according to which he can manipulate modern history. But Soustelle's political failure is less problematic for Naipaul than the question of the relation of life to art, history to myth, fiction to non-fiction. He notes that in interviewing Soustelle,

> He still seems able to survey his experience with wonder; he seems continually to process and refine this experience as it expands within its defined limits. It is the method neither of the scholar nor of the politician, but of both together; and it comes close to the method of the novelist, making art of egotism, creating a private impenetrable whole out of fragments which from a distance might appear unrelated (p. 209).

And later:

> This playing with the idea of defeat appears also to come from the Soustelle who makes art out of his experience and who now, in exile, has discovered all the consonances of this experience. The politician has known defeat; the

> ethnologist has studied a defeated people (a recent letter has told him that the Lacandones are in danger of extinction); the study of ethnology itself derives from a civilization that is on the defensive. The pattern, too neat, belongs to art. It is art, though, that comes close to self-indulgence (p. 216).

It is precisely this ambiguous relation between art and life, between history and myth, which informs much of Naipaul's later writings.

Whatever it is about Steinbeck, Mailer and Soustelle that empowers them as subjects to become originators, to become creative links in the cycle of myths that make up Western culture, is lacking in the post-colonial societies of "Columbus and Crusoe." Rather than subjects engendering their own myths of origin, they are objects, present or past, which political powers manipulate in the exercise of their subjectivity. Not unlike the "India" section, these societies are perceived by Naipaul in terms of their engagement with the colonizing West, even when this is past. The aftermath of colonialism and slavery is as devastating as its actual practice.

In all six essays, the societies in question are trapped within their lack of a myth of origin (Anguilla, the exception, nurtures the myth of being a shipwrecked community, which is, in fact, a myth of non-origin) on which to construct themselves as subjects. Colonialism and its instrument, slavery, which resulted in both a physical and a cultural dislocation, constructed societies whose existence was conditional on serving either as a projection or as an object to subdue. Thus the only way Naipaul can discuss these societies is in this relation: British Honduras as a colony caught between two powers; St. Kitts as an ex-slave society in which the instability of the political ideological base is reflected in the comic strip character of party names—PAM and WAM; Anguilla, as the mouse that roared, a tiny island which had the audacity to cede from the British Commonwealth and posed such a threat that it had to be recolonized; Trinidad and Jamaica as "manufactured societies, labour camps, creations of empire" (p. 275);[17] and Mauritius, "an agricultural colony, created by empire in an empty island and always meant to be part of something larger, now given . . . independence and set adrift, an abandoned imperial barracoon, incapable of economic or cultural autonomy" (p. 292).

The ex-slave societies of "Columbus and Crusoe" have no canon of written text against which to test their reality or on the basis of which to create a history. Thus the texts that they engender, and upon which Naipaul bases his articles, although myth producing, are all of the transient, shifting present, and all hinge on the dynamics created by colonialism and its consequences: oral testimonies, songs, advertisements, social studies, etc. As Paul Berenger, the founder of the Mauritian MMM says: "'They all deal in fantasies. And it's rooted in the colonial situation'" (p. 308).

The Overcrowded Barracoon as a Marginal Autobiography

In her theory of autobiography, Elizabeth Bruss successfully avoids the dichotomy between self as an ontological problem and genre as form by shifting the locus of the autobiographical impulse to an act, and translating the idea of form into functions. Bruss sees the task of autobiography theorists as explaining how "there can be both change and continuity in autobiographical writing, and frame our explanation in a way that will not distort individual autobiographies."[18] Her solution is to turn to linguistics and the philosophy of language, to the work of Austin, Searle and Strawson, for a concept that will serve. Autobiography, like other genres, she claims, is an illocutionary action, i.e., "an association between a piece of language and certain contexts, conditions and intentions"[19] which is recognizable within a particular community of readers and writers. "Just as speaking is made up of different types of actions carried out by means of language, the system of actions carried out through literature consists of its various genres."[20] Nevertheless, Bruss finds it possible to describe "limited generalizations . . . about the dimensions of action which are common to these autobiographies, and which seem to form a core of our notions of the functions an autobiographical text must perform."[21] These generalizations, which pertain to the relationship of the subject who writes and the product, the work itself, are narrowed down to three basic rules: 1. The autobiographer is the source of both the subject matter and the structure found in his text: "a) The author claims responsibility for the creation and arrangement of his text. b) The individual who is exemplified in the organization of the text is purported to share the identity of an individual to whom reference is made via the subject matter of the text";[22] 2. The information and events recorded in an autobiography are asserted to be the case, the author claims so and the reader accepts this; 3. The autobiographer himself believes what he asserts.[23]

These rules necessitate, Bruss goes on to say, that

> the nature of the man or woman writing, the stance and voice adopted within the text, and the features of the emerging characterization must converge, to qualify or even contradict each other, since all are within the specified scope of the autobiographical act. Moreover, the shape into which these various aspects of the act coalesce is by definition that of a personality, a self, an identity; it must have, as Blake might say, 'a human face' whether the author or reader is ultimately responsible for imposing it.[24]

While Bruss's discussions of individual autobiographies in the second half of her book focus on the relationship of the autobiographical act to the language in which it is embedded, they are not ultimately concerned with the self that generated the act, or with the relationship between self and act. That such an act of self writing took place is taken for granted. What is examined is what form such an act takes in particular cultural, historical contexts.

The Overcrowded Barracoon problematizes Bruss's theory not because it challenges the rules she sets down but precisely because it conforms to them. Although obviously not conceived consciously as an autobiography, and while most of the essays were written during a period when Naipaul's autobiographical impetus was channeled into intellectual pursuits, the retrospective selection and ordering of the material is so directed by the drive, the quest for self, which underlies all of Naipaul's works, that the book becomes what could be called a marginal autobiography. The result is to highlight the instability of the boundaries between autobiography and other genres, a condition brought into self-conscious play by many postmodern writers as a means of commenting on both the art of fiction and the fictiveness of self. Naipaul will demonstrate his intellectual engagement with these postmodern ideas in *The Enigma of Arrival* where they converge with his search for new modes to construct his post-colonial self.

In one sense the book is an extreme manifestation of the non-subject. The mode—a selection of newspaper and magazine articles and book reviews, spanning almost fifteen years—is one of disconnected units of writing of varying lengths, on a variety of subjects and covering numerous geographical locations, with a multiplicity of referents and an inconsistent use of the narrating "I," told in shifting tenses. Not only is there a focus on multiple referents that draws the reader's attention away from any possibility of exploring the autobiographical subject, but the language itself, conventional and "transparent," facilitates our immediate engagement with the topic of each article.

This explicit level of the book confirms Naipaul's overt intentions at the time. The problem of the split self and the loss of origin (still explored in the first section of the book) gives way to an engagement with intellectual—social, historical, political—preoccupations and a life of roaming which temporarily sets aside the need for place. And yet, the retrospective ordering and organization of the essays in the book strongly reflects the autobiographer who is "the source for the structure to be found in his text," and who "claims individual responsibility for the creation and arrangement of his text," just as the selection (both as noun and as action) of articles in the collection, whether conscious or otherwise, very much demonstrates Bruss's stipulation that "the individual who is exemplified in the organization of the text is purported to share the identity of an individual to whom reference is made via the subject matter of the text." As the analysis in the previous section has shown, it is Naipaul, the travelling writer, who is both the source of the subject matter of the text and the one to whom reference is made via the subject matter of the text, even or perhaps especially when he is virtually absent from it.

The articles are presented almost without exception in chronological order of writing in each section, with overlapping between the sections. The essays of the first section are thus the earliest and the essays of the last section are the latest, and, in addition to the interest inherent in each article, one is made aware of an overriding concern to make possible the emergence of a development, a sequence of thought or attitude on the part of the writer over the period of time covered.

Furthermore, the articles are grouped into four, separately titled sections, the dates of articles in one section overlapping with those in others. These thematic groupings again reveal the mind of the retrospective author analyzing and ordering his earlier experiences into broader thematic frameworks, indicated by the titles (two of which are drawn from the articles themselves and two invented for the collection). The overlaps in dates between one section and another suggest other possible groupings (for example "Cricket" and "Jamshed into Jimmy" written in the same year have a common thematic base—the adoption by the colonized of the culture of the colonizer) but clearly Naipaul is not interested in presenting his experiences in sequence or in groupings which would emphasize thematic links between the explicit subjects of the articles, but in organizing them so that they reflect the themes of his own experience and development as he perceives them at the time of selection.

This organization is reenforced by the titles of the sections: "An Unlikely Colonial" and the entire first section represent a point of departure for the period covered by the book as a whole. The qualifier "unlikely" destabilizes the epithet "colonial," hence throwing into focus the shifting ground under Naipaul's grasp of origin; "India," involving actual voyages to the East, represents Naipaul's attempt to recover his origins in his lost ancestry; "Looking Westward" explores the reciprocity of history and writing or myth-making in the West, and, as the title implies, suggests a desired goal combined with the position of being an outsider; and "Columbus and Crusoe" evokes two originators, mythic figures, historical and fictional.

As already mentioned, throughout *The Overcrowded Barracoon* a pattern emerges concerning the relationship of the narrating "I" to the subject matter of the text. In the first two sections of the book this is a strong link: in the first section the "I" *is* the subject matter and in the second, the "I" is felt as a strong emotional presence, although diminishing throughout the section. At the same time these sections deal explicitly with the "non-I" which is the result of the encounter between colonizer and colonized, usurper father and stepchild, and is Naipaul's point of departure when he begins his travels. Conversely in the second half of the book, while the narrating "I" almost completely disappears as a presence, to the extent that he refers to himself in some articles as "the visitor" or the "visiting writer," the subject matter of the two sections represents in transposition the splitting of the subject in relation to origin: "Looking Westward" dealing with the position of the Western writer as a myth maker vis-à-vis the relationship of myth to reality and the past; and "Columbus and Crusoe" dealing with the colonized, the "dark" side of the split subject after the encounter with the alien father.

To call the source of autobiography an autobiographical act is both to focus on and to obscure the problem of intention. Do the expression of underlying personal structures, themes and the perhaps unconscious retrospective ordering and selection of material in a certain pattern constitute autobiographical acts? If so, are we not then in danger of attributing autobiographical intentions to almost any written text? *The Overcrowded Barracoon*, by playing out these and other questions, shows Naipaul driven to seek a mode to express the quest for self, at a time in his life when the means to do it were least evident. The decades of travel, which *The Overcrowded Barracoon* documents, acted in a way as an unconscious "working through" from the myth of non-origin to the possibility of finding origin within oneself.

CHAPTER THREE

In a Free State

In a Free State[1] has been the subject of a broad spectrum of critical scrutiny, ranging from the purely existential,[2] through comparisons with Conrad's *Heart of Darkness*,[3] to the vociferously ideological which scourges Naipaul for his alleged contempt for Africans and his so-called neocolonialism. My own very specific interest in *In a Free State* within the overall project of tracing Naipaul's evolution into autobiography is as a fictional counterpart to *The Overcrowded Barracoon* (which was published at approximately the same time). *The Overcrowded Barracoon*, I have shown, enacts the state of the non-self characteristic of Naipaul's middle phase, both through the intellectual quest to comprehend the relationship between history, myth and origin in the colonial and post-colonial world, and through the biographical fact of ceaseless travelling. It gathers together many of the themes and issues which concerned Naipaul in this period, creating a sense of the split self severed from a myth of origin as the driving force of the book, at the same time as it demonstrates the disunity of self through the assemblage of disparate essays. Finally, while it exemplifies Naipaul's turning to non-fiction as a viable narrative mode parallel with but separate from the fiction he was writing at this time, it reveals his growing awareness of history as a fictional construct.

In a Free State provides a kind of fictional mirroring of many of the same issues. As a collection of two stories and a novella framed by a journalistic Prologue and Epilogue, its pose is of a work which does not quite cohere into a whole. At the same time, the short pieces in it are linked by theme: all of the protagonists enact the state of displaced people undergoing or having undergone a journey, suspended in an ambiguous state of "freedom" not unlike that of Naipaul himself, and reveal a rupture between life in the symbolic order and myth of origin. *In a Free State* in many ways echoes the themes of its fictional predecessors, *The Mimic Men* (1967) and *A Flag on the Island* (1967), and anticipates those of *Guerrillas* (1975) and *A Bend in the River* (1979), thus serving as a kind of middle point in Naipaul's fiction. But it is its transitional structure that is most interesting here. By framing the work with two entries from a journal, Naipaul not only introduces the author in a status equal to that of his fictional characters, but also plays with the idea of incorporating biographical/historical material into his fiction. The resultant blurring of the boundaries between the two modes hints at Naipaul's search for a way to grant the historical a place in fiction and vice versa.

The framework of *The Overcrowded Barracoon* is travelling. The journey becomes both the source of narrative and the manifestation of a psychic state. Similarly, but cast in a fictional mode, in *In a Free State* "The journey is, in fact, the book's central metaphor."[4] This is true not only of the protagonists of the stories within the book, but also of the narrator of the journalistic Prologue and Epilogue, purported by most critics to be Naipaul himself. But just as in *The Overcrowded Barracoon* the journeying captures the suspension between a life of freedom, an attempt to create a life in the symbolic order unfettered by the past, and the quest for origin, so in *In a Free State* the characters are, as Linda Anderson has declared: "people who have abandoned their native lands and live in places where they are no longer in accord with their surroundings. They are casualties of freedom because they are suspended between these two states, unable to cope with self-knowledge, yet no longer innocent."[5] While in *The Overcrowded Barracoon* the intellectual project is used to compensate for and give direction to the sense of non-self, the characters of *In a Free State*, crippled and trapped within their own insufficiency, can express only rage and helplessness. Incapable of engaging as subjects with the culture within which they find themselves, and unable to merge with it as with the lost origin, they are free yet paralyzed, unable to move either forward or backwards, exiled from self.[6]

Self vs. Origin

Both Santosh, the protagonist of the first short story, "One out of Many," and the unnamed narrator of "Tell Me Who To Kill" are products of colonial or ex-colonial societies; for each, the creation of an identity is contingent on abandoning the past which offers no future and struggling to find a substitute existence in the West. Uprooted from his native Bombay and transplanted in Washington, D.C., Santosh is aware of the past, the lost myth of origin, as a state of belonging, but also of non-differentiation: "I was once part of the flow, never thinking of myself as a presence" (p. 57). Like Lacan's infant, Santosh then "looked in the mirror and decided to be free" (p. 57). The split which Lacan accords to each individual is here, as it is with Naipaul, bound up with a double loss: of origin and, through the cultural displacement, of myth of origin. Yet, paradoxically, it is the displacement itself, the entrance into the alien symbolic order, which precipitates the emergence of subjectivity, however incomplete. Thus the original culture, as in the case of Naipaul himself, is experienced as not being able to confer a sense of self. Severance is vital, but the loss cannot be accommodated by the substitute culture. Once he has gained the symbols of the alien order, moving from the purchase of a green suit to the acquisition of the precious green card, Santosh turns his back to the wall: "I have closed my mind and heart to the English language, to newspapers and radio and television . . . . I do not want to understand or learn any more" (p. 57). Santosh's evolution into subjectivity is at once a birth and a death. On the one hand he progresses from living in the womb-like security of a cupboard to being master of his own room, on the other his freedom is experienced as an emptiness, a death: "To be empty is not to be sad. To be empty is to be calm. It is to renounce" (p. 55). To be a presence is thus to confront absence. It is interesting to compare the sense of death in this story to death as it will be experienced in *The Enigma of Arrival*, Naipaul's personal coming into presence. Whereas here death is the symbol of absence, a force that denies self, in the later work the acquisition of a sense of self includes the acceptance of death as part of presence.

Another facet of Santosh's thwarted bid for selfhood is his connection and finally marriage with a black, a *hubshi* in his language. For Naipaul, blacks, whether in Africa, in Washington, or India, are closely linked with origin. As the recipients of the whites' repressed fantasies of aggression,[7] they come to represent the instinctual part of the self, a symbol of regression. In Santosh's original culture, it is said, "it is indecent and wrong for a man of our blood to embrace the *hubshi* woman" (pp. 34–35). The marriage with the black woman thus represents a succumbing to the very forces which threaten the self acquired through the symbolic order, and recalls Naipaul's fear of sinking into non-differentiation on his first visit to India as described in *The Overcrowded Barracoon*. This fear extends to the story in its entirety in which the rioting of the blacks of Washington is depicted like the eruption or liberation of a destructive, latent force threatening to engulf "civilization" in flames.

During his early wanderings through the black-dominated streets of Washington, Santosh observes what he describes as half-caste Hindus dancing in praise of Lord Krishna:

> I was very pleased. But then a disturbing thought came to me. . . . I thought that these people were now strangers, but that perhaps once upon a time they had been like me. Perhaps, as in some story, they had been brought here among the *hubshi* as captives a long time ago and had become a lost people, like our own wandering gipsy folk, and had forgotten who they were (p. 30).

This is a direct reversal of the legend related in *The Overcrowded Barracoon* of the conquest of India by the Aryans, of whom Santosh is a descendent, and the subjugation of the native "Darks." In the manner of all conquests, the natives become a repressed dark centre, origin or other. In Washington, D.C., however, in the process of losing self, the taboos of the subjugated get violated. The marriage to a *hubshi*, like the riots, is a form of regression for Santosh which does not yield freedom. Once again, the story demonstrates that for Naipaul's subjects, at least at this stage, while there is no possibility of coming to terms with the adopted culture, a retreat back to a pre-subject stage is also not the answer.

In "Tell Me Who to Kill," the problem of the entrapment between the abandoned past and the alien culture is rendered through a splitting of consciousness between the narrator and his brother. It is the brother Dayo who assumes the role of entering the alien symbolic order, encouraged by the narrator, by leaving his native West Indian island to receive an education in England. The apparently quiet resignation with which he fails in his educational endeavours and finally buys an entrance ticket to Western society by marrying a white girl is offset by the narrator's state of perennial rage and sense of futility. The narrator becomes that part of consciousness—a fixation on the impoverished past, the continued perception of the alien culture through fantasy engendered by films, and the rage of helplessness—which must be "killed off" and left behind as the price of admission into the new world:

> And now my brother come to me. He is going away with his wife, for good. He hold me by the hand, he look at me, tears come in his eyes, and he say, 'I love you.' It is true, it is like the time he cry and say he didn't have confidence. I know that he love me, that now it is true, but that it will not be true as soon as he go out of this room, that he will have to forget me. Because it was my idea after my trouble that nobody should know, that the message should go back home that I was dead. And for all this time I am the dead man (p. 102).

The narrator's "trouble," a violent outburst against the dregs of English society that provoke him simply because he is "Other," is in fact a kind of self-annihilation, resulting in his dependency on "Frank," the kind white man who now leads him by the hand: "Frank is sitting beside me on the bus now. I am on the inside, looking down the road. He is on the outside, pressing against me" (p. 97). Finally, then, the relationship between the colonial child and the alien father remains the same. The brother will live in the alien culture having severed himself from the most meaningful part of himself, and the narrator reverts to the condition of non-self engendered by the encounter between the colonial and the usurping power. For neither is there a future.

In this story, the voyage to England by ship represents the narrator's insertion into the alien symbolic order which is, in fact, a shift from one non-existence to another:

> I don't want the ship to stop. . . . I can't go back, I will have to stay. I don't know how I trap myself. . . .
>
> The mystery land is theirs, the stranger is you. None of those houses in the rain there belong to you. You can't see yourself walking down those streets set down so flat on that cliff. But that is where you have to go . . . This is it, and already you are like a man in blinkers. I tell myself I come to England to be with Dayo . . . .
>
> I watch the season change from cold to warm. I manage, I am all right, but only because I feel it is not my life. I feel as I feel on the ship, that I lose that, that I throw that away (pp. 79–80).

Not only does this journey echo Naipaul's own voyage to England, but it will be used again in *The Enigma of Arrival*. In "Tell Me Who to Kill" it stands as a symbol of rupture that is not understood by the protagonist and can lead only to impotence and rage, whereas in the later work the recognition of the split self makes the journey part of a cycle which includes both ends and beginnings.

If "One Out of Many" and "Tell Me Who to Kill" delineate the disastrous consequences to the creation of a subject of the attempt to enter into the symbolic order of the alien father, a voyage of darks in the white world, the title novella, "In a Free State," describes the reverse: the thwarted quest of the incomplete subject, in this case two white people, to recover origin in a symbolic journey through black Africa. Bobby and Linda's journey by car through an African state in political turmoil to the haven of the British Protectorate in the south represents, in the words of Linda Anderson, "An attempt to recapture an innocence which existed in a past it is impossible to reenter."[8] But the confrontation with Africa, the journey inwards which in many ways echoes Marlow's journey in *Heart of Darkness*, yields not a moral horror in which the self comes face to face with the evil within (and which, in fact, confirms the inherent boundaries of self) but the horror of absence—the emptiness, hollowness of the split subject who, in a quest for wholeness, can reproduce only the reverberations of his/her entrapment in a particular version of the symbolic order. Origin, in the shape of Africa, either beckons or erupts in a chaos which language (at least that of the whites) cannot contain.

Africa, to the protagonists, is the seat of yearning for completeness, a primal condition. It is a place which fosters the illusion that one can recover a lost sense of wholeness:

> This was the famous view. This was the openness the sky had been promising. The land dropped and dropped. The continent here was gigantically flawed. The eye lost itself in the colourless distances of the wide valley, dissolving in every direction in cloud and haze. . . .
>
> 'It's absurd,' Bobby said, when they were sitting in the car again, 'but I feel all this'—he indicated the great valley—'belongs to me' (pp. 116–117).[9]

Both protagonists are emotionally damaged people for whom the geographical dislocation is the outer manifestation of an internal condition. Both feel estranged by their original culture, England, and cut off from their past, and although their "symptoms" are defined mostly in sexual terms (Bobby is homosexual and Linda a "man eater"), their preoccupations, especially those of Bobby, are existential. Bobby's past is a breakdown, a retreat from subjectivity, which was "like watching yourself become a ghost" (p. 116), or "A wish to give up, to be nothing, to do nothing" (p. 153). In Africa he seeks the pre-verbal narcissistic mirroring in homosexual relations: "Sweet infantilism, almost without language: in language lay mockery and self-disgust" (p. 109). Linda's identity, on the other hand, is determined by the vicissitudes of her husband's public role as program writer for the BBC (and the propagandist role it suggests), a series of transfers through false, temporary havens, further and further away from an authentic existence:

> He asked, 'Where do you think it'll be?'
>
> He waited.
>
> She said, 'South.' (p. 126).

While Bobby represents the liberal white who identifies with Africa and Africans and is capable of seeing intellectually beyond his own cultural imprints, Linda is saved from being a mere white supremacist "compound wife" only by her sexual activities which make her too an object of gossip, and by a bitter intelligence that occasionally breaks through her bigoted veneer: "'As Martin says, the only lies for which we are truly punished are those we tell ourselves'" (p. 160). Each enacts a version of the incomplete self, Linda by maintaining an imperviousness to any kind of change that could threaten to penetrate the brittle symbolic order she inhabits, Bobby by making an active, though mostly unconscious attempt to recover origin. Both are locked in their insufficiency and for both the exposure brought on by their African experience is ultimately a futile exercise. The self that is the product of the symbolic order recognizes its lack, yet origin is unattainable.

If in "One Out of Many" and "Tell Me Who to Kill" the protagonists grow into a split subjectivity suspended between a lost past and an alien "Other" culture, in "In a Free State" Bobby and Linda are incomplete selves in confrontation with "Other" (Africa) as origin. As a landscape it is, as Linda puts it, "pre-man," as a society it is (to their Western eyes) non-rational, chaotic, violent and mysterious. But to allow oneself to be engulfed by it, as Bobby does, and to lose the covering of selfhood acquired culturally at great cost is to self-destruct. For, as Naipaul leads us to understand in this phase of writing, while without a myth of origin there can be no experience of self, there is no subjectivity outside the symbolic order.

I have chosen two of the thematic strands that make up the story to illustrate the point. One is that of violence, external and internal, and the other is language—the set of linguistic and cultural signifiers which create the world Linda and Bobby inhabit. These are inversely related: as the violence looms ever nearer the protagonists until it overtakes them and erupts, language increasingly loses its efficacy to act either as a means of communication or as a barrier against chaos.

The violence in "In a Free State" is both an objective fact—the hunting down of the king by the president's men—and an experience of invasion by the Other and the losing of the boundaries of self. The story plays on the prejudices and vulnerability of the reader by blurring the distinction between the actual danger and a kind of violence that Bobby provokes, making them finally converge. The political events which precipitate the danger surround Linda and Bobby like the ubiquitous helicopter that drones overhead. However, the ominousness of the relations between the whites and the Africans during the journey seems to increase concomitantly with, or as the result of (we are never sure which), Bobby's gradual exposure of his insecurity, his lack of identity and his quest for oneness. In each successive confrontation with Africans one experiences a growing dread from both the external events and from Bobby's unconscious flirtation with the danger. But the irony of the gap between Bobby's idea of Africa and his ultimate punishment is not only political. It is the failure of the split subject to recover origin.

The African country Linda and Bobby are riding through is in the grip of tribal warfare, a struggle between a king and a president, presented by the narrator in the tone of the opening of a fairy tale: "In this country in Africa there was a president and there was also a king" (p. 103). Neither is named, and the struggle, beneath the increments of modern technology, seems to be taking place, at least as far as Bobby and Linda are concerned, on a primitive, non-verbal level, with shades of patricide recalling Freud's imaginings of the origin of culture in *Totem and Taboo.*[10] The struggle itself is to their Western eyes purposeless and lacking in reason, thus reverting to an unnameable "African" quality. The Africans are perceived as performing secret savage rites, and the capture of the king by the opposing tribe is fantasized by Bobby and Linda in terms of a primitive hunt:

> She said, "I saw a dead leopard once."
>
> Bobby concentrated on the road.
>
> "In West Africa. A long red tongue hanging down from between the teeth... Then they began to skin it. Just below the skin it was like a ballet dancer in tights. You wouldn't believe the muscles. All that had to be cut up and thrown away, burnt on the fire. In the morning when I got up I thought, 'I'll go and look at the leopard.' I'd forgotten."
>
> She spoke slowly. She had begun to listen to her own words.
>
> Bobby said, "I don't believe they're going to skin the king" (p. 216).

Nature in Africa is a primal force, not only moulding and remoulding the landscape but insidiously wiping out the comparatively meagre achievements of Western civilization:

> A forest stream, it turned out, with the forest debris of collapsed trees. But from the high bank on which he stood Bobby saw flat stones and boulders below the raging red water: stepping stones: the small thrills, perhaps, of an ordered garden in a gentler season. A little way up there was a remnant of a retaining brick wall. The stream had long ago breached that and now in flood was making another channel through what had once been a garden (p. 131).

It is within this primitive, secret force that Bobby seeks to make himself whole. But each encounter with Africans demonstrates just how futile the attempt is. The inner need which drives Bobby's behaviour inevitably results in a misreading of the reality. He seems at once understanding and naive about the motives and intentions of the Africans he comes into contact with (it is always Linda who strikes a realistic, albeit racist, note), as if Africa *can* be assimilated into oneself. At the same time the means which he brings to achieve this merging are, and can only be, cultural, the signifiers of the symbolic order—his language, his vulnerability expressed in alternations between imperialist cliches: "How dare you turn your back on me while I'm addressing you?" (p. 148) and an absurd attempt to make his language fit theirs, resulting in the collapse of his speech into pidgin: "'You no have curfew?' Bobby said" (p. 230).

No event better metaphorizes the relationship between the incomplete self and the Other as origin than the episode of the dogs. Here Linda and Bobby come closest to experiencing both the pre-verbal world of Africa and the dangers to self such an experience can produce. Walking down the boulevard of a semi-abandoned ex-colonial resort town being reclaimed by Africans, they seem to return to a time before "civilization:"

> 'It's funny,' Linda whispered, 'how you can forget the houses and feel that the lake hasn't even been discovered.'
>
> 'I don't know what you mean by discovered,' Bobby said, not whispering, 'The people here knew about it all the time.'

> 'I've heard that one. I just wish they'd managed to let the rest of us know' (p. 187).

The exchange captures the essence of the problematic relationship not only between colonizer and colonized, but also between white and African as a metaphor for subject/origin. Linda at first acknowledges the existence of a feminine pre-discovery, pre-naming world which Bobby grants as a myth of origin to the local inhabitants. But her second remark qualifies that recognition by making its existence contingent on a linguistic process. Besides demonstrating once again the usurpation of language/history from the indigenous population by the colonizing factor, it also suggests that for Bobby and Linda any acquisition of that primal world can only come through the signifiers of their own culture.

But the possibility of entering a pre-verbal world endangers subjectivity. Straying off the lit boulevard into a darkened street, Bobby and Linda are gradually surrounded by a pack of hostile dogs:

> A dog barked, a low deep sound; and then it was beside them, big and growling. They walked on, the dog shepherding them angrily past his lot. Dogs barked on either side of the road ahead. And soon they were walking between dogs that obeyed no boundaries. . . .
>
> 'Oh my God,' Linda said. 'These dogs don't have any owners. They've gone wild' (p. 188).

In these moments, which are out of time, they come face to face with a world in which cultural signifiers have lost their stable meaning. A world without boundaries is a world of chaos, invasion, incorporation. Appropriately enough, the incident brings to Linda's mind Bobby's earlier recounting of the experience of being bitten by his mother's dog and being scarred for life—a hint, perhaps, of the price Bobby has paid for his quest. And, interestingly, it is rage rather than fear that characterizes Bobby's reaction to the incident—perhaps the remnant of an infantile rage toward the insufficient mother.

Following the incident Bobby sits alone at the bar: "The anger turned to exhaustion, and melancholy at his own solitude, in that bar, beside that vast African lake" (p. 190). For the incomplete subject, the final state is solitude—looking upon origin but unable to merge with it.

As the protagonists travel further south and deeper inward, Bobby's quest moves inexorably towards its inevitable crisis. His final and fateful encounter with the Africa of his journey seems to enact his unconscious motives:

> His instinct was to get back in the car and drive without stopping to the compound. But he controlled himself. Quickly, right hand swinging, he crossed the bright road into the dusty yard and the shadow cast by the stone building, and went through the open door.
>
> As soon as he entered he knew he had made a mistake. But it was too late to withdraw (p. 229).

The beating to which he is subjected seems gratuitous—displaced rage on the part of the Africans. But for Bobby it is more than an attack which "he had half understood, half felt sympathy." It is an event in which he *becomes* an African in a complete reversal of roles:

> 'Boy!'
>
> He [Bobby] stopped; it was his error. He turned, to face the dark room (p. 231).

And when his wrist is shattered: ". . . he could have cried then, at . . . the knowledge that what had been whole all his life had been broken" (p. 232). The rhetorical weight of this sentence suggests that the break is not merely physical; it is, perhaps, the moment of the recognition of the irreversibility of the split in the subject. And, indeed, at the end of the novella, when Bobby reenters the British compound, he reassumes his role of English master: "Bobby thought: I will have to sack Luke" (p. 238).

As Bobby (with Linda on the sidelines) is pulled further and further towards a confrontation with Africa, language, the signifying system which shapes the self, increasingly loses its effectiveness to contain the experience.

At the start of the journey the use of language reflects the precarious state of the incomplete subject in the world:

> A sign said: BEWARE OF FALLEN ROCKS.
>
> 'That's one of my favourite road-signs,' Bobby said. "I always look for it.'

'So precise.'
'Isn't it?' (p. 115).

Language is also inadequate to serve as a means of communication: "He was stilled. She could find nothing to say." Or later in the same episode: "They had both seen the view many times and neither of them wanted to say anything that the other might have heard before or anything that was too fanciful" (p. 116).

The strongest role language plays in the early part of the story is to reinforce Bobby and Linda's relationship with the white world, the symbolic order, through an endless storehouse of clichés ("They are restless today") or punning:

> 'What is it our Duchess says?'
> 'Duchess?'
> 'That's how I call her.'
> 'You mean Doris Marshall?'
> 'I bend over "black-wards." Isn't that what she says?' (p. 118).

But the scope of language to contain and express a variety of emotions is limited: "She looked at her lap and whispered, 'It's pathetic.' If she uses that word again, Bobby thought, I'll hit her" (p. 146).

Finally, as the boundaries of self slowly dissolve, the power of language to hold and confer identity disappears. One significant example is Bobby's use of pidgin in a vain attempt to communicate with the Africans, an act which not only completely divests him of the little identity he has but which gives him, from the outside, the air of being condescending and probably contributes to the violent attack against him. Another expression of the destabilizing of language as the conveyer of cultural codes occurs in the use of identical phrases in contradictory situations. At the hotel Bobby tries to pick up Carolus, the young black waiter. In a hostile confrontation Carolus demands the money Bobby has promised him even though he has not rendered the required service, as Bobby sees it:

> 'You give me.'
> 'Give you? Give you nothing. Give you whip.'

> It wasn't even true; it was someone else's words; he was violating himself. . . .
>
> He said, 'I give you. I promise you. I give you' (p. 196).

The phrases rebound on Bobby in the scene of the beating. Here, the roles are reversed. Bobby relinquishes his language with his self to the African who toys with him:

> 'I give you cigarette boy.'
> 'I no smoke,' Bobby said.
> 'I give you. Come. I give you' (p. 231).

Bobby's desire for the gift of love in the earlier scene is thus replaced with the gift of physical violation in which his quest culminates, conflating the inadequacy of the symbolic order with the self annihilation inherent in the quest for origin.

Freeing the Genre

To this assortment of displaced characters in different settings Naipaul added a frame, a Prologue and an Epilogue, consisting of two pieces entitled journal entries. These entries have been accepted by the majority of scholars as non-fictional testimonials, taken from an authentic journal kept by the author Naipaul himself.[11] By complementing the thematic strands of the stories, the journal pieces bring their narrator in direct relation to the characters he has invented. In the Prologue, the narrator, on a ferry crossing to Egypt, acts as observer and commentator to the humiliation of a tramp, a non-belonging "other," by the other passengers. In the Epilogue, the narrator shifts from the role of witness to an act of degradation to the active role of one who intervenes. In an act which he recognizes as futile, he stops the ritualistic whipping of Egyptian beggar children for the entertainment of the tourists.

To many scholars, the transition from observer to participant on the part of the narrator signals a significant shift in Naipaul's position from outsider and fence-sitter in the Western world, to one committed to action. As Landeg White sees it, for example: "Nothing is achieved when Naipaul seizes the camel whip. But the sudden clarity, the sense of outrage, the decision to act—all these are positive in that they define a concern which the writer cannot abrogate. The impulse to act has become the impulse behind his writings."[12]

I would like to use this transition as a metaphor for an analogous process—Naipaul's gradual development from the sense of non-self as it is manifest in his writing from the second phase, to his active creation of a myth of origin and a hybrid narrative mode in the third. It is a transition which separates the characters of *In a Free State,* including the passive narrator of the Prologue, from the narrators of *Finding the Centre* and *The Enigma of Arrival* who seek to understand and finally to correct their condition. I believe this movement is apparent in *In a Free State* not only on the symbolic level but also in the structure and the narrative mode, in what Morris has called the dissolving of the shadow line between reality and fiction.[13]

The incorporation of authentic journal entries into a work of fiction creates a link, I have said, between the situation of the journal writer, Naipaul, and the themes arising from the fictional pieces in the book. The alien position of all the fictional protagonists in the book is echoed in the tramp meticulously observed by the narrator in the Prologue. And even more emphatically is Bobby and Linda's quest for origin reiterated by the narrator in the Epilogue in his musing on the ancient art of Egypt:

> Perhaps that had been the only pure time, at the beginning, when the ancient artist, knowing no other land, had learned to look at his own and had seen it as complete. But it was hard, travelling back to Cairo, looking with my stranger's eye at the fields and the people who worked in them, the dusty towns, the agitated peasant crowds at the railway stations, it was hard to believe that there had been such innocence (p. 246).

By framing the stories with the journal entries, Naipaul, then, could be signaling to the reader that his fiction should be read in relation to his biography. At the same time, the intrusion of the non-fiction on the fiction seems to indicate that for Naipaul the fictional mode alone, unlike *The Mimic Men,* which was written as a "straight" fictional autobiography, is no longer adequate to express his autobiographical drive.

Yet a closer scrutiny reveals that there is, in fact, nothing in *In a Free State* to attest to the fact that the journal entries are indeed what they are taken to be. On the surface they certainly imitate diary entries: The narrating "I" records his observations and his own actions meticulously and dispassionately. The entries have no overt structure, no beginning and, more importantly, no end. In that, they seem to suggest the ongoing flux of reality characteristic of journal writing. There are also signs linking the narrator to Naipaul—his extensive travelling, his fastidiousness, etc. At the same time, the narrator is never named, and the pieces are entitled "Prologue, from a Journal," "Epilogue, from a Journal", suggesting anonymity. Furthermore, their style suggests a retrospection and a distancing atypical of the diary mode: "It was only a two-day crossing from Piraeus to Alexandria, but as soon as I saw the dingy little Greek steamer I felt I ought to have made other arrangements" (p. 7). There is also no extra-referential information, such as a declaration of intent, a date, a name, to suggest that these journal entries are anything but fictional constructs appearing in a book of fiction.

This is the beginning of Naipaul's active undermining of the fictional mode in his quest for a narrative form to serve as a vehicle for his autobiographical drive. The work is a fiction into which the referential has been projected as a possibility. Only in his third phase, beginning with *Finding the Centre* and coming to fruition in *The Enigma of Arrival*, does Naipaul develop the implications of this experiment for the writing of autobiography. There he reverses the relations between the two modes. While in *In a Free State* the historical is introduced as a component of fiction, in the works of the third phase fiction becomes a component of history.

CHAPTER FOUR

Finding the Centre

Finding the Centre[1] constitutes a turning point in the writings of V. S. Naipaul. It is the first work of what I have called the third phase, during which Naipaul resolved both his lack of a myth of origin and the problem of form in his autobiography *The Enigma of Arrival*. But *The Enigma of Arrival* could not have been written without *Finding the Centre*, which serves it, as the title of the first narrative suggests, as a prologue.

In this study I have thus far attempted to trace two parallel threads constituting the split in Naipaul's writing life. One, the life-as-writer in the alien language and culture parallel to the insertion into the symbolic order of the colonial usurper, and two, the quest for the severed past, the lost myth of origin. The first saw the exploration of the realm of the word in its different manifestations, and the second comprised the preoccupation with place as a displacement of the quest for mother/father/myth of origin.

The second phase of Naipaul's writing, while on the one hand perpetuating the split through the multiplicity of "places" visited, analyzed and thematized as part of the life-as-writer, on the other acted as a subtle working through in terms of both the author's understanding of the problem of origin and finding the appropriate narrative mode for autobiography. The intellectual investigations of the relationship between history and myth, including the attempt to recover his own history by rewriting the history of the region of his birth in *The Loss of El Dorado*, brought with it the awareness that origin, denied in the early phase and sought in the second phase, was in fact a myth of origin, a creation.[2] The results of this gradual shift constitute the third phase of Naipaul's writing, the phase of resolution culminating in his coming into self and autobiography through the creation of his own myth of origin in *The Enigma of Arrival*.

The achievement of *The Enigma of Arrival*, however, necessitated a crucial, prior act: the confrontation with the past, the lost myth of origin, as void. Whereas in his earlier works the confrontation took the form of denying the existence of a myth of origin (for example by inventing the myth of non-origin), here it becomes a recognition of the inevitable repudiation of the myth of origin under the conditions of his colonial upbringing. Only when the severance from the myth of origin is made complete by this self-knowledge can the act of creating one's own myth of origin be conceived. *Finding the Centre* is the narrative of the arrival at that self-knowledge.[3]

As the prologue to but not the autobiography itself, *Finding the Centre* continues to enact Naipaul's split at the same time as it attempts, and to a large extent succeeds, in getting to the bottom of the problem. In its composition *Finding the Centre* perpetuates the split, each of its two non-fictional narratives embodying one of its aspects: "Prologue to an Autobiography," as an exploration of the symbolic order as a means to create self, and "The Crocodiles of Yamoussoukro," as a quest for origin in its displacement onto place. At the same time *Finding the Centre* moves towards self-knowledge by confronting the absence that is at the centre of the quest for origin while examining the ways in which language, written and oral, facilitates that discovery. By holding a reckoning with earlier, chiefly fictional, modes of dealing with the past, namely *A House for Mr Biswas* and the story "Bogart,"[4] Naipaul traces his writing ambition back to its origins as a legacy from his father who also bequeathed him his void. Furthermore, the links between "Prologue to an Autobiography" and "The Crocodiles of Yamoussoukro" undermine their expository, factual modes of discourse, foreshadowing the particular relation of fact to myth, or fiction to non-fiction, brought to fruition in *The Enigma of Arrival* and comprising Naipaul's narrational solution to the writing of autobiography.

"Prologue to an Autobiography"

Where the classical autobiography traditionally begins with the birth of the writer (often a very difficult birth, almost leading to the death of the hero before he begins to live), "Prologue to an Autobiography" begins with a description of the birth of the first sentence of Naipaul's first "publishable book." The sentence, "Every morning when he got up Hat would sit on the banister of his back verandah and shout across, 'What happening there, Bogart?'" (p. 16), is not only a pivot on which memory is transmuted into fiction, it is also evocative of the sentence in *A House for Mr Biswas* with which the hero, Mohun Biswas, is obsessed: "Amazing scenes were witnessed yesterday when—" (p. 211). This sentence in its non-completed form represents Mr Biswas's state of mental arrest, of nightmarish entrapment and yet of standing on the verge of the word. His major breakthrough into the world of journalism, a world which at least initially seems to provide a place of inhabitation for the self, is accompanied by a feverish completion of this sentence in his mind. Naipaul's first "publishable" sentence in many ways echoes that earlier one. It is an interrogative sentence demanding a reply and hence a completion. The question asked, "what happening" implies a witnessing or even involvement and a desire to hear a report of a scene. And the asking of the question is a recurring event: "Every morning . . .", an unremitting ritual. Its completion is the beginning of Naipaul's life-as-writer.

The question that Naipaul is putting to himself in "Prologue to an Autobiography" is to what extent the life-as-writer makes a self. He is, in other words, attempting to investigate the power of writing to reveal or, if that is impossible, to substitute for a myth of origin. In order to answer that question Naipaul embarks on a kind of autobiography of the writing life, a process of spiralling down to the centre, which is an abyss where, as in *A House for Mr Biswas*, he and his father converge. The movement towards the centre, towards self-knowledge, is at the same time a movement backwards, a tracing of the shifting ground under memory, fiction and fact, and the fluid boundaries between them. Three constitutive elements of Naipaul's writing life are considered in "Prologue to an

Autobiography": the immediate surroundings represented in the character of Bogart, Seepersad Naipaul's writing career and Naipaul's relation to it, and the family and community history. In all three spheres, the sources of writing are initially apprehended through memory; this faculty turns out to be unreliable, the agent of a fictionalizing process which, in order to reveal the centre, must be defictionalized. The process occurs both in the life-as-writer and, as we would expect, in the narrative itself. And in all three cases it is developed through motifs of entrapment and escape. The Bogart in the story spun out of childhood memory "wished to be free" (p. 20), but "looking only for freedom . . . [he] had ended up as a man on the run" (p. 21). The real Bogart, encountered twenty-seven years later, "had lived the life of freedom, and it had taken him back almost to where he had been in the beginning" (p. 48). The family origin, originally conceived as a black hole of darkness, "impossibly remote, almost as imaginary as the land of the *Ramayana*, our Hindu epic" (p. 52), is revealed to have been formed round the suspension between the old world of India and the new world of Trinidad. To Naipaul's grandfather, "Trinidad was the interlude, the illusion" (p. 52), and he attempted to escape by returning to India, while for Naipaul's father, as a child, to escape was to hide in the latrines and refuse to return to India.

But the chief example of defictionalizing in "Prologue to an Autobiography" involves Naipaul and his father's legacy of the writing ambition, which is examined through an implicit comparison between the writing of "Prologue to an Autobiography" and that of *A House for Mr Biswas*. In "Prologue to an Autobiography" Naipaul feels the need to "set the record straight" concerning his father's writing career in the light of certain facts that came to his attention as an adult, and in so doing he makes a comparison between this new vision and his earlier, formative conception of his father's writing. This comparison is not limited to the content of the different perceptions, but is also very much concerned with the narrative modes they gave rise to: the early model which produced the deflected autobiographical novel, *A House for Mr Biswas*, and the mature understanding which is the writing of "Prologue to an

Autobiography." Thus the movement out of conflict into knowledge which this narrative augurs also pertains to narrative mode.

The first part of "Prologue to an Autobiography" recounts Naipaul's childhood memories of his father's writing career which fueled his own early writing, from "Bogart" to *A House for Mr Biswas*. The second half of the narrative is concerned with a correction of that childhood vision: the discovery that just when he was moving towards an independence created out of his journalism, his father was forced to sacrifice a goat, seemingly to appease the goddess Kali but in reality to surrender to his tradition-bound powerful family whose cultural heritage he had rejected. This act opened up an abyss, the erasure of the most primal idea of self: "He looked in the mirror one day and couldn't see himself. And he began to scream" (p. 70).[5] Naipaul realizes that his father's recovery, all his subsequent work, was ". . . fear of extinction." And this was also his legacy: "That was his subsidiary gift to me. That fear became mine as well. It was linked with the idea of the vocation: the fear could be combated only by the exercise of the vocation" (p. 72). For both Naipaul and his father the writing career was conceived not only as an escape but as a way to create self. However, in the absence of a myth of origin, the centre which fueled Naipaul's writing ambition is revealed to be a received void. Thus Naipaul's split repeats his father's split and explains the ambivalence with which his attitude towards his father is fraught. The identification, evidenced not only in the writing career itself but also in the incorporation of Seepersad Naipaul's stories into his own work, is counteracted by the rejection, the escape, from Trinidad, the conscious abandonment of the family and especially his father in an act of repudiation: "And it was with that sudden churlishness, a sudden access of my own hysteria, that I had left my father in 1950, not looking back. I wish I had" (p. 39).

The consideration of *A House for Mr Biswas* as a yardstick against which self-knowledge in "Prologue to an Autobiography" is measured occurs on several levels. Naipaul regards his writing as an ascending movement towards knowledge. Thus all his previous books, *A House for Mr Biswas* among them, are proclaimed deficient: "Beginning a book, I always felt I was in possession of all the facts about myself; at the end I was always surprised. The book before always turned out to have been written by a man with incomplete knowledge" (p. 28). (This in fact calls into question the status of "Prologue" itself.) And with regard to *A House for Mr Biswas,* he says:

> This was, very roughly, what I knew when, two years after I had written about Bogart and the life of the street, I thought of reconstructing the life of someone like my father. . . . The book took three years to write. It changed; and the writing changed me. I was writing about things I didn't know; and the book that came out was very much my father's book. It was written out of his journalism and stories, out of his knowledge, knowledge he had got from the way of looking MacGowan had trained him in. It was written out of his writing (p. 63).

The above quote suggests not only that *A House for Mr Biswas* was written along the lines of an autobiographical novel in its power to exorcise or reorder the past ("and the writing changed me"), but that it was written in a kind of repetition of his father's way of writing in the *Guardian.* Furthermore, while Naipaul earlier on has claimed that "book by book . . . I eased myself into knowledge" (p. 27), he also claims that "the book before always turned out to have been written by a man with incomplete knowledge" (p. 28). This links Naipaul with the character of Mr Biswas whose journalism is a search for a way to inhabit reality through the word, to create and order reality. Naipaul wrote *A House for Mr Biswas,* he claims now, as his father wrote journalism—a method which both in *A House for Mr Biswas* and in real life could not ultimately substitute for self.

The writing of *A House for Mr Biswas* and "Bogart," then, is linked with Naipaul's false idea of his vocation as a writer of fiction in the grand English tradition, to be resolved and corrected by the end of "Prologue" not only with the discovery of the true facts and the ensuing insight into the true foundation of his career, but in the blend of fact and dramatization which is the narrative mode of "Prologue to an Autobiography" itself.

The structure of "Prologue to an Autobiography" reinforces this view. The state of greatest self-knowledge achieved by the end of the narrative is compared to the state of deficient self-knowledge set forth in its first two chapters, which use the same background material that served as the source for the writing of "Bogart" and *A House for Mr Biswas* (incomplete, as it later transpires). The first chapter recounts the "facts" that went into the writing of "Bogart": "That was Bogart's story, as I knew it" (p. 19). Chapter Two serves a double purpose: it recapitulates Naipaul's formative childhood confrontation with his father and his father's writing, and the foundation of his own adoption of the vocation of writer, but in so doing it also retells a major part of the plot of the second half of *A House for Mr Biswas.* Reading Chapter Two of "Prologue to an Autobiography" is, in fact, like reliving an important part of the novel.

Suffice it to draw a number of parallels: the period in Port of Spain recounted in Chapter Two when Naipaul first makes the acquaintance of his father's ledger and his writings, and of the pieces of furniture that had been accumulated until then, corresponds to the first two chapters of Part Two of *A House for Mr Biswas*; the move to the cocoa estate parallels the Shorthills adventure in Chapter Three of Part Two of the novel, and life back in Port of Spain with most of the extended family crowded into his grandmother's house, corresponds to Chapters Four and Five. Newspaper stories written by Naipaul's father and read in his ledger are the material for Mohun Biswas's first journalistic attempts, and family politics in real life are modified to represent the background of Mr Biswas's reportages.

But the parallels are also a matter of evocation: for example, in "Prologue to an Autobiography" Naipaul refers to his father before the Port of Spain period as a vague figure in his life:

> He must have been in the house, though; because in the subsidiary two-storey wooden house of the back of the main building there were—on the inner wall of the upstairs verandah—jumbled ghostly impressions of banners or posters he had painted for someone in my mother's family who had fought a local election. . . . The glory, of the election and my father's banners, belonged to the past; I accepted that (p. 30).

This strongly recalls Savi's idea of her father in *A House for Mr Biswas*:

> And at Arwacas, the shop signs celebrated snow and Santa Claus . . . Mr Biswas's old signs still served. They had faded; . . . near the ceiling the lettering was dim with dust and soot. Savi knew, and was proud, that the signs had been done by her father. But their gaiety puzzled her; . . . she felt, with a sense of loss that became sharper as Christmas drew nearer, that the signs had been done at some time beyond her memory when her father lived happily at Hanuman House with her mother and everyone else (*A House for Mr Biswas*, p. 212).

Similarly, Mr Biswas's occupation and preoccupation with sign painting and lettering is transmuted to Naipaul himself in "Prologue to an Autobiography": "Just as I had inherited or been given a feeling for lettering, so now. . . ." (p. 31).

Thematically, a comparison of the rendition of a crucial event in "Prologue to an Autobiography," the father's breakdown, with the equivalent scene in *A House for Mr Biswas* brings the growth in self-knowledge into even sharper focus. In *A House for Mr Biswas*, written in 1960, Mr Biswas's breakdown occurs as a result of the hopelessness and frustration of his life before he becomes a journalist. Journalism is thus seen as the cure, the yearned-for life in the word that can provide a haven (temporary and unsatisfactory as it turns out), and a self. The breakdown is fictionally enhanced into a climactic, turbulent event. The house Mr Biswas had built with inferior materials is disintegrating around him. Anand, whom he has tried to claim and initiate into his inner world, is terrified. A storm breaks out. Mr Biswas is slowly going out of his mind, unaware of his surroundings. And the difference in self-awareness between Mr Biswas and Naipaul in "Prologue to an Autobiography" is not accidental. The house is overcome by the force of the wind and rain and the light goes out:

> Then there was a roar that overrode them all. When it struck the house, the window burst open, the light went instantly out, the rain lashed in, the lightning lit up the room and the world outside, and when the lightning went out the room was part of the black void.

> Anand began to scream.
> He waited for his father to say something, to close the window, light the lamp.
> But Mr Biswas only muttered on the bed and the rain and wind swept through the room . . . and forced open the door to the drawing-room, wall-less, floorless, of the house Mr Biswas had built.
> Anand screamed and screamed (*A House for Mr Biswas*, p. 292).

As already noted elsewhere,[6] this scene marks the juncture of Anand's and Mr Biswas's stories. As Mr Biswas sinks into the oblivion from which he will emerge as a writer, Anand experiences the void with him. Thus in Naipaul's fictionalizing of the relation of writing and self, Anand with his scream takes on both the reversion to the pre-language void and the subsequent "cure," the adoption of the alien symbolic code.

In 1972 Naipaul discovered that his father's breakdown occurred *after* the peak of his journalistic career, following the enforced sacrifice of the goat and the departure of his Western mentor, MacGowan, the editor of the *Guardian*. Naipaul writes of his father's account of his humiliation that, on the morning following the sacrifice, "My father, in his own report . . . has very little to say. He has no means of recording what he felt" (p. 70). Thus in his real life, journalism, i.e., the alien symbolic order, could not lift him permanently out of the past he had rejected, nor could it provide him with a self that could act as a substitute for that lost past. His father's recognition becomes Naipaul's own awareness of the lack at the centre of his writing life (demonstrated by "Prologue to an Autobiography"), a lack that does not allow for the sense of self or the possibility of writing autobiography. Yet, whereas in *A House for Mr Biswas* it is Anand who screams in identification with his father's experience, in "Prologue to an Autobiography" Naipaul returns the scream to his father. His confrontation with the void and its repetition in himself is self-conscious, but it is most of all dispassionate, separate. It is the first step on the way to becoming a self.

A second aspect of the process of defictionalizing in "Prologue to an Autobiography" is the implied privileging of certain types of texts, what I would call documentation, over others. In *A House for Mr Biswas* Mr Biswas spends his days moving from one type of life in the word to another, from sign painting, to journalism, to social survey writing, and so on, in order to find a viable existence for himself, but it is chiefly through his abortive attempts at the writing of fiction and poetry that he comes closest to bringing the lost past into the realm of the word. In "Prologue to an Autobiography" Naipaul portrays his life-as-writer as a moulding of experience into different kinds of narrative modes: the short story, the novel, travel accounts, and history, but it is clearly the "factual" documentations of the later stage—testimonials, letters, history books, telegrams, newspaper clippings, etc.—that are the instruments of insight. In his illuminating interpretation of the relation of documents to fiction in Naipaul's work, Peter Hughes writes:

> Excerpts from letters and police ledgers anchor fantasies in the historical world, which is oddly more literary than fiction in its compulsory appeal to written records. The novelist can appeal to the reader's sense of how we experience the world, to some shared notions of human nature, but the historian and his narrative are tied to records, to a second and second-hand nature out of which he has to create the illusion of a first-hand nature, until the account of how it really happened merges into an illusory proof *that* such things really happened.[7]

At the same time, while each testimonial is a step forward in the gaining of knowledge, it is also, paradoxically, a peeling away of yet another layer of words from the centre which is language-less. The symbolic order can take him only to the edge of origin which always remains a void.

"The Crocodiles of Yamoussoukro"

If "Prologue to an Autobiography" investigates the choice and substance of the life-as-writer only to discover the absence that the parallel severance from a myth of origin created at its centre, "The Crocodiles of Yamoussoukro," a travel account, reflects the way the quest for the absent myth of origin permeates the symbolic order, the life-as-writer. The centrality of the life-as-writer as a substitute for self is also exemplified by the relations each of the two texts suggests between self and text.

In "Prologue to an Autobiography," text or writing, in all its forms, serves as both framework and tool for an active project of coming to an understanding of what Naipaul calls his "literary beginnings" (p. 9), which is, in fact, the autobiography of the writing self, the only "self" available to him. "The Crocodiles of Yamoussoukro," on the other hand, traces a seemingly passive process whereby the life-as-writer becomes narrative: "So while, when I travel, I can move only according to what I find, I also live, as it were, in a novel of my own making, moving from not knowing to knowing, with person interweaving with person and incident opening out into incident" (p. 87).

The preoccupation with place as the translation of the quest for a myth of origin, a thread traceable in Naipaul's works from *A House for Mr Biswas,* exists in "The Crocodiles of Yamoussoukro" on two levels: narrative mode and theme. As a travel account, "The Crocodiles of Yamoussoukro" embodies that condition of no-place characteristic of Naipaul's middle phase, the almost ceaseless wandering over the globe as journalist/writer. His father's, or Mohun Biswas's, restless journalistic wanderings and quest for house are transmuted in the adult Naipaul into the life of the universal outsider who says about his travels: "I go to places which, however alien, connect in some way with what I already know" (p. 87).

Ostensibly a true account of a journey to the Ivory Coast, "The Crocodiles of Yamoussoukro" develops thematically around the quest for origin and at the same time offers metaphoric reinforcement of the issues of "Prologue to an Autobiography." Yamoussoukro is a place where "the ancestral village has in fact vanished from public sight. The entire village—huts (if they still survive), common ground, the semi-sacred palavar tree—has been incorporated into the grounds of a new presidential palace. And all is hidden by a high palace wall that must be many miles long" (pp. 75–76). The "gut" place, the centre of this country's history, which represents the heart of all Africa, has been incorporated into a modern palace. Naipaul's trip to the Ivory Coast thus corresponds to his journey to his writing centre, and the obstacles on the way to visiting Yamoussoukro, the people he deals with—Africans contaminated by the West, European expatriates, West Indians in Africa—are like so many aspects of himself to be peeled away, like the layers of culture, of civilization, like the layers of words in "Prologue to an Autobiography."

Africa itself has an active primal quality for Naipaul. As seen in *In a Free State*,[8] it is a place where the inroads made by Western civilization and colonialism are always in danger of being overcome by the bush, by the erupting power of some untamable force that obliterates all man's efforts at "art":

> . . . Africa can often seem to be in a state of becoming. It is always on the point of being made something else. So it arouses hope, ambition, frustration, irritation. . . .
>
> And then at a place like Yamoussoukro, where the anxiety becomes most acute, it also begins to feel unreal. You get a glimpse of an African Africa, an Africa which . . . has always been in its own eyes complete, achieved, bursting with its own powers (p. 77).

Africa's aura of completeness and origin explains the fragility and tenuousness of the hold that Western imperialism, a kind of global alien symbolic order in its own eyes, can have. The whole superstructure of civilization in the Ivory Coast seems like something that could disappear overnight. This extends from government projects down to the waiters at a restaurant: "The waiters, impeccable the day before, were casual, vacant. . . . Someone was missing, perhaps the French or European manager. And with him more than good service had gone: the whole restaurant-idea had vanished. An elaborate organization had collapsed" (p. 129). The difficulty exists in the other direction too. Ebony, the young African poet, was told by his father that he was being educated not to become a white man but to enter the new world. The new world, says Naipaul, "existed in the minds of other men. Remove those men; and their ideas—which after all had no finality—would disappear" (p. 130).

Besides its metaphoric quality as a kind of universal origin, Africa has served as a concrete myth of origin to the displaced black peoples of the world. "The Crocodiles of

Yamoussoukro" examines the relation of several such displaced people to this myth of origin which is Africa.

Despite the claim for so-called randomness in the development of encounters and events in this narrative, the people who interest Naipaul most, and whom he has chosen to write about, are those who, like himself, are doubly displaced—once, having grown up as a transplanted minority in a colonial society, and then again by removing themselves from that society and, as in the case of the characters of "The Crocodiles of Yamoussoukro," seeking a reunion with their severed myth of origin. The most poignant examples are of black West Indians who have come to live in Africa: "But when I had thought of going to the Ivory Coast, I hadn't thought of French West Indians making the roundabout journey back" (p. 90). The verdict concerning this attempt, in Naipaul's eyes, is unanimous. None has succeeded in returning to Africa as to origin. And although each has found his or her individual solution to the condition, they are all expatriates in the land of their myth of origin. Furthermore, within this land, "true" origin, the "African Africa," remains inaccessible to them. And in this they repeat Naipaul's insight as described in "Prologue to an Autobiography": the rejected myth of origin is permanently severed and cannot be refound.

At the same time, it is interesting to distinguish among the attitudes toward this irrevocable condition revealed by the different characters. For, as Naipaul will show in *The Enigma of Arrival*, the solution is up to the creative efforts of the individual. For Arlette, the black West Indian divorced from her African husband, living in Africa means separating herself from the patronizing preconceptions of French West Indians and finding a *modus vivendi* within her own solitude: "And it was also clear that, in spite of her failed African marriage and her present solitude, there was in her some deep feeling for the Africa that followed its own ways" (p. 92). For Andree, another expatriate West Indian, home continues to be and will always be the colonial French Guadeloupe of her upbringing. Young Busby, whose father was a Barbadian who went back to Africa, lives in England and keeps alive the crusade for the dignity of the black man. But, says Naipaul, his cause "was a private cause, from another continent, another past, another way of looking and feeling" (p. 110). To the double expatriates, Naipaul adds the ordinary kind, the Englishmen and Americans who come to Africa to fill some central lack in themselves, and on all he pronounces the same judgement: "Africa called to people for different reasons. Everyone who went and stayed had his own Africa" (p. 141).

The centre that these characters seek, however, is, like Naipaul's own centre, inaccessible. Covered over by the achievements of the acquired Western culture, the highway, the hotels and the golf course, it is a mythologized unknown that belongs to the heart of Africa which is governed by night and by sorcery and is guarded by man-eating crocodiles, those totemic creatures which once again evoke the killing of the father and Freud's *Totem and Taboo.* To recapitulate, Freud's mythic description of the beginning of Western society depends on an act of the killing of a father by rival sons, an act which is transformed into a taboo which forms the basis for kinship and incest laws. This framework also serves as the underpinnings of Lacan's symbolic order, the product and substance of language, the place of inhabitation of the subject. The crocodiles that guard the hidden ancestral village at Yamoussoukro are man-eating creatures whose potency as would-be castrators is vividly documented in the ceremony of feeding:

> The chicken lost control of its neck, which hung limp. Two old crocodiles, as though used to the ritual, waited close together on the sand. . . .
>
> A shout from the crowd told me that the chicken had been thrown. And when I turned I saw the bird turned to a feathery debris in the seemingly grinning maw of one crocodile, not the oldest, round unseeing eyes apparently alight with pleasure, black feathers sticking out on either side of the jaw (p. 134).

The fear of castration, the reversal of the desire to kill the father, at the gates to the fiercely guarded, forever lost primal existence, once again merges personal and cultural origins. And just as in *A House for Mr Biswas* the father's death is accompanied by an act of incorporation causing Mr Biswas his lifelong stomach troubles, here at the same boundary between the symbolic order and the repressed myth of origin, is the fear of being devoured. The return to origin is associated with the loss of self, incomplete as it may be. And it is perhaps no accident that so much of "The Crocodiles of Yamoussoukro" occurs around meals, so fastidiously described that we sense that Naipaul's stomach is no less sensitive than that of his father/Mr Biswas.[9]

The evocation of *A House for Mr Biswas* is also evident in the description of the mythic ancestral village of Yamoussoukro: "—huts (if they still survive), common ground, the semi-sacred palavar tree" (p. 75) which recalls Mohun Biswas's half-remembered, half imagined sensations "of an evening meal being cooked over a fire that shone on a mud wall and kept out the night, of cool, new, unused mornings, or rain muffled on a thatched roof and warmth below it: sensations as faint as the scent of the *poui* itself, but sadly evanescent, refusing to be seized or to be translated into a concrete memory" (*A House for Mr Biswas*, p. 174). Unlike Mr Biswas's clinging to that ideal, however, it is Naipaul's recognition that this myth is not only untranslatable but no longer his own, that will lead the way to his solution to the problem of autobiography writing in *The Enigma of Arrival* through the creation of his own myth of origin.

Fiction vs. Narrative Design

Clearly, in *Finding the Centre*, the two aspects of the split subject, existence within the symbolic order and the lost myth of origin, while giving rise to analogous themes, still operate as separate functions, as evidenced by the separate narratives. However, the links which I have shown between them suggest a movement not only towards the thematic integration of the two parts but also towards the evolution of a narrative mode to contain that integration.

Both "Prologue to an Autobiography" and "The Crocodiles of Yamoussoukro" are based on verifiable fact, and are thus consistent with Naipaul's shift away from the fictional mode in the quest for self expression.[10] However, the "cohabitation" of these two narratives under one book cover creates narrational connections between them that, while not obliterating their factualness, supersede them.

I have said that "The Crocodiles of Yamoussoukro" thematizes the concerns of "Prologue to an Autobiography," namely, the quest for the lost myth of origin and the final severance from it. In so doing, the events described in "The Crocodiles of Yamoussoukro," whose factuality is emphasized by the narrator's passivity in controlling them, acquire an additional, metaphoric function. The thematic meaning is thus created through a metonymic relation, through a system of differences, to borrow a Saussurian term. Rather than create an imaginary, fictional world as a vehicle of meaning, Naipaul can translate the thematic creation of a myth of origin into a narrational solution by manipulating facts into a system of meaning, a narrative design.[11] This mode, which in *Finding the Centre* remains suggested rather than fully implemented, will reach its culmination in *The Enigma of Arrival*.

CHAPTER FIVE

The Enigma of Arrival

The Enigma of Arrival[1] is Naipaul's myth of origin and the autobiography of his post-colonial self. It is a work in which language, through its very manipulations, strives to become the nonlanguage of primary experience. At the same time, it is a work of highly sophisticated artifice, the *record* of the creation of a myth of origin, i.e., a creation in language, and the resolution in terms of genre of the problem of writing autobiography. The protagonist is both Naipaul, a writer and traveller of international renown, the facts of whose writing life are known and verifiable, and an unnamed, coming-into-existence being who is inserted into the cycle of history, life and death. *The Enigma of Arrival* thus encapsulates the battle over origin fought in such peculiarly twentieth-century terms: while it lives the yearning for origin anterior to language which conditions our existence, and especially the concept of self and autobiography, the work acknowledges its only conception as a sign within the signifying chain of language symbols. Thus it fulfills the condition of a myth of origin whose in-built contradiction is constitutive of self.

The insoluble contradiction between the act of creating in language and the thing it wishes to create—origin—informs *The Enigma of Arrival* not only at the level of the actual use of language, but also thematically, structurally and in terms of genre, and it is around these four axes that this chapter will attempt to engage Naipaul's project.

Theme: "The Enigma of Arrival"

Early in the section "The Journey," the narrator recounts a story (told in at least two versions) he has fantasized from a reproduction of a painting by Chirico, given the title "The Enigma of Arrival" by the poet Apollinaire. The story, the narrator acknowledges, is in fact a *mise-en-abyme* of his own life story, and by extension, of *The Enigma of Arrival* as a whole: ". . . years after I had seen the Chirico picture and the idea for the story had come to me, again, in my own life, was another version of the story of 'The Enigma of Arrival'" (p. 97), and "It did not occur to me that the story that had come to me as a pleasant fantasy had already occurred, and was an aspect of my own" (p. 157).

The story "The Enigma of Arrival" is of interest here in two ways: one, as the thematic axis of the book *The Enigma of Arrival* and two, in terms of genre (which will be considered in the last part of this chapter), for it illuminates the relation of "truth" and "fiction" in Naipaul's creation of a myth of origin.

Thematically, the story-within-the-story serves as a paradigm of the cyclical process whose final realization has been the writing of *The Enigma of Arrival*. The dictionary definition of the various uses of the word "arrival" may serve as a useful point of departure: To arrive: 1) To reach a destination: to come to the end of a journey; 2) To make an appearance: to come on the scene; 3a) To gain or achieve an end, especially by conscious effort: to attain or reach a state of mind or position. . . . 3b) To reach or come to a stage of development especially by the passage of time. . . . (OED).

The dictionary definition immediately pinpoints a paradox contained in the concept: arrival as the reaching of a destination and arrival as the appearance on a scene—an end and a beginning, a death and a birth. Each side of the paradox also contains its opposite: to appear on a scene implies purpose, destination, whereas arrival as the reaching of a destination suggests an appearance which is also a beginning. It is the very paradox which informs Naipaul's creation of a myth of origin, and, by extension, his autobiography which is *The Enigma of Arrival*. For Naipaul, the writing of an autobiography, the creation of a myth of origin in writing, can only take place when death and beginnings meet and converge at the place of arrival. The encounter with Wiltshire, the early months in the cottage there, is represented in "Jack's Garden" as a joining with, an assimilation, almost an absorption into, a primal, pristine landscape: ". . . the sense of space was overwhelming" (p. 15)[2]; "It was possible on this stretch of the walk to hold on to the idea of emptiness" (p. 15); a complete, permanent world: "Here was an unchanging world—so it would have seemed to the stranger. So it seemed to me when I first became aware of it" (p. 34). A sense of the beginning of all learning: "I saw what I saw very clearly. But I didn't know what I was looking at. I had nothing to fit it into" (p. 12).

As a creation of a myth of origin, it feeds on two needs: one, to acquire a myth of a *cultural* origin and two, to have that cultural origin constitute a place, a signifier for repressed fantasies of primal yearnings, i.e., to reconcile (in Lacanian terms) the Name-of-the-Father, Law, history and the mother—the landscape.

Naipaul's Wiltshire experience supplied both. The cottage is near Stonehenge, the earliest evidence of history in England, which becomes linked with the idea of space:

> The emptiness, the spaciousness through which I had felt myself walking was as much an illusion as the idea of forest behind the young pines. All around—and not far away—were roads and highways, with brightly coloured trucks and cars like toys. Stonehenge, old barrows and tumuli outlined against the sky; . . . The old and the new; . . . (p. 15).
>
> Daily I climbed up from the bottom of the valley to the crest of the way and the view: the stone circles directly ahead, down below, but still far away: grey against green, and sometimes lit up by the sun. Going up the grassy way (and though willing to admit that the true processional path might have been elsewhere) I never ceased to imagine myself a man of those bygone times, climbing up to have this confirmation that all was well with the world (p. 23).

This primal experience, as I have said, integrates the two hitherto separate parts of Naipaul's being: "I could find a special kind of past in what I saw; with a part of my mind I could admit fantasy" (p. 22); "Though I hadn't truly seen those views before or been in their midst, I felt I had always known them" (p. 38). And, "The solitude of the walk, the emptiness of that stretch of the downs, enabled me to surrender to my way of looking, to indulge my linguistic or historical fantasies; and enabled me, at the same time, to shed the nerves of being a stranger in England" (p. 23). The narrator's symbolic order—represented by literature—is inserted into the history of the place:

> So the idea of antiquity, at once diminishing and ennobling the current activities of men, as well as the ideas of literature enveloped this world which—surrounded by highways and army barracks though it was, and with the clouds in the sky sometimes seeded by the vapour trails of busy military aeroplanes—came to me as a lucky find of the solitude in which on many afternoons I found myself (p. 24).

(Note how, grammatically, the modern industrial world is enveloped, swallowed almost, by dashes, in the sentence.)

The assimilation into this completeness is accompanied by a dual, ultimately mutually destructive process. The first is the process of learning, the gradual awareness of otherness as distinct from self. In Naipaul's case, the acquisition of knowledge proceeds from a discarding of a "linguistic" pre-knowledge of the place culled from education ("I knew that 'avon' originally meant only river . . ."), through the above described sense of emptiness and beginning, to a slow awareness of the surroundings:

> But it took some time to see the garden. So many weeks, so many walks between the whitish chalk and flint hills up to the level of the barrows to look down at Stonehenge, so many walks just looking for hares—it took some time before, with the beginning of my new awareness of the seasons, I noticed the garden (pp. 20–21).

The process of learning, however, is necessarily the occasion, as in childhood, of the loss of the ideal, wholeness and completeness. "And beside Jack's garden, Jack's hedge: a little wall of mud-spattered green, abrupt in the openness of the droveway, like a vestige, a memory of another kind of house and garden and street, a token of something more complete, more ideal" (p. 21). "In this way of seeing at that time what I wanted to see I was a little like Jack's father-in-law, who ignored the new fence that cut at many places into segments of his 'run' across the droveway" (p. 27). Knowledge must gradually admit to change and decay, the permanent giving way to the transient, hence, origin overlaid by mutability. Sights are constantly revised as learning grows: "Yet I had taken the house for granted; in the gradual shaping of the land around me, the neat house had taken longer to come out at me, to be noticed. The antiquity—so much vaguer, so much a matter of conjecture—had made its impression more easily: I was ready for it" (p. 30). Or, "I had thought of him as a young man. But I saw now that his beard was almost grey; he was in his late forties, perhaps" (p. 32).

But most of all, the creation of the myth of origin is inevitably accompanied by the acknowledgement of death:

> . . . and those sturdy green fence posts . . . and the taut lines of barbed wire made me feel, although the life of the valley was just beginning for me, that I was also in a way at the end of the thing I had come upon. . . . These ideas, of a world in decay, a world subject to constant change, and of the shortness of human life, made many things bearable (p. 26).

To acquire a self in the sense of accepting the fact of one's birth is to accept what Freud has termed "the pressure towards death."[3]

The book opens with an illness that gives way to a healing process which constitutes the narrator's rebirth into the English landscape. However, the cycle of the narrator's stay at the manor cottage comes to an end with another illness, which, unlike the first, foreshadows old age and death. In other words, the culmination of the period in the valley is the eruption of his own decay: "It was with real illness now, a more than passing incapacity, a fatigue that seemed to have gone beyond the body to the core and motor of my being . . . it was with true illness . . . that I began . . . to take short turns in the sodden, ruined manor garden" (p. 299). And yet, the *writing* of *The Enigma of Arrival* requires the completion of an even greater cycle, one that will include the lost past of childhood. This occurs in the final section of the work, the record of the death of the narrator's sister in Trinidad, his journey there and his participation in the Hindu rites marking her death. The experience in Wiltshire, ending with illness and a foreshadowing of death, led to a new beginning in the converted cottages, accompanied by "a great melancholy," "thoughts of death, the end of things" (p. 309). But it is only his sister's death that can transform the convergence of end and beginning in the narrator's life cycle into an arrival that makes the writing of *The Enigma of Arrival* possible:

> . . . the sacred places of our childhood . . . I had lived in them imaginatively over many books and had in my fantasy set in those places the very beginning of things, had constructed out of them a fantasy of home, though I was to learn that the ground was bloody. . . . Every generation now was to take us further away from those sanctities. But we remade the world for ourselves; every generation does that, as we found when we came together for the death of this sister and felt the need to honour and remember. It forced us to look on death. It forced me to face the death I had been contemplating at night, in my sleep; it fitted a real grief where melancholy had created a vacancy, as if to prepare me for the moment. It showed me life and man as the mystery, the true religion of men, the grief and the glory. And that was when, faced with a real death, and with this new wonder about men, I laid aside my drafts and hesitations and began to write very fast about Jack and his garden (p. 318).

The writing of the book is in itself, of course, also a new beginning, a new cycle.

To the ontological paradox of the concept of myth of origin, "Jack's Garden" and the other Wiltshire sections thus add another dimension: the becoming of self as inexorably bound up with the end of self.

Structure: to Be Inserted into Origin

The story-within-a-story "The Enigma of Arrival" contains, in fact, two arrivals. In the first, the young man arrives at a port, in search of a destination, but for some unnamed purpose, a beginning. In the second, the arrival back at the quay, the man is searching for a beginning, but in fact has reached an end. What links both arrivals is the repetition, the return to the same place, which traces the trajectory of a cycle. What distinguishes them is knowledge. The first is in a sense a false arrival because it is not perceived to be one; the second becomes a "true" arrival by dint of the self-knowledge that transforms it from an end into a beginning. The cycle is framed by two beginnings: one, the origin of the journey by ship, which, although implied, is lost and shrouded in oblivion, and the last, the beginning that is the traveller's recognition that the ship has sailed and his life is "played out," that what he has to look forward to is death.

It is not difficult to apply this structure to the life depicted in *The Enigma of Arrival.* The book has five sections. Three are concerned with the narrator's sojourn in a cottage on an estate in Wiltshire, the time of his "rebirth," which spanned ten years of his life; another, "The Journey," is a record of the narrator's writing life up to and including the period of rebirth; and the final chapter records an event, his sister's death, taking place in Trinidad after his departure from the cottage. The pattern which informs the three chapters on Wiltshire is not one of chronology, a single time sequence, but of space, in which many cycles, of nature, decay and birth, flux, life and death, history, love and hate, marriage and divorce, are ongoing simultaneously. The section "The Journey," in contrast, although constituting a cycle by beginning and ending in the present, is in fact a linear narrative recording time before Wiltshire as a sequence of events connected with writing.

The insertion of the section "The Journey" into the sequence of the "cyclical" sections on Wiltshire is a structural representation of the incorporation of the pre-Wiltshire existence into the rebirth at Wiltshire. This culminates a process both in the narrator's life and in the strategy of the narrative as the creation of a myth of origin. It also focuses on the opposing tensions inherent in such a creation.

In one sense the insertion of a linear, sequential narrative of the narrator's life-as-writer into a group of narratives where the linear progress of time is rendered irrelevant, endows the

Wiltshire experience with a sense of primal timelessness, an experience taking place outside of time. Seen this way, it appears that, biographically speaking, the narrator's life is working towards a kind of regression, which is the birth into his "second life" (p. 159). It is the linear "writer's life" that must disintegrate in order for the new life to begin.

There are many indications of this in the section itself. It opens, as noted, with illness, an illness brought on by an obscure malady of the nerves, exhaustion and disappointment, the fruits of the narrator's life-as-writer:

> . . . the unknown Wiltshire; the cruelty of this return to England, the dread of a second failure; the mental fatigue. All of this, rolled into one, was what lay on the spirit of the man who went on the walks down to Jack's cottage and past it. Not an observer merely, a man removed; but a man played on, worked on, by many things (p. 96).

The illness is represented by a recurring nightmare in which the narrator is awoken by an explosion in his head, and is brought on by the narrator's recognition of the falseness of the identity base provided by the life-as-writer. A book commissioned by a publisher, which had caused the narrator to dismantle the life in England built up over eighteen years to go travelling back to his native region with the personalized history he has written about it, falls through; he is forced to return to England to what he recognizes as the non-life there: ". . . that journey back to England so mimicked and parodied the journey of nineteen years before, the journey of the young man, the boy almost, who had journeyed to England to be a writer, in a country where the calling had some meaning, that I couldn't but be aware of all the cruel ironies" (p. 95).

The falseness of the identity assumed in the original conception of his life-as-writer is given further symbolic representation at the end of the section in the letter from Angela, a figure from his early time in England, which arrives "almost at the end of my time there" (p. 159). Angela, an immigrant like himself, unable to pronounce the narrator's name, and in an attempt no doubt to find a common ground between them, had at the time of their first acquaintance renamed him: "She called me Victor" (p. 159). Now ten years into his "rebirth," the irony of that act is acknowledged: "And it worked for me, too: through all the intervening sensualities, all the uses to which I had put my body, the name Angela had given me called up the enigma and false promise of that early time in London . . ." (p. 159). It should also be noted that *V* is the first initial of Naipaul's own given name.

Though the career of the writer has flourished, the life-as-writer elaborated and fleshed out, the underlying structure thus appears to be hollow, and must be destroyed to construct a new base, the foundation that is given to him at the cottage. It is therefore not surprising that the biographical events focused on in "The Journey" are (with the exception of the frame which includes the present) those of the writing career, the life without a myth of origin, the same life-as-writer whose false origins were explored in "Prologue to an Autobiography."

The description begins with the narrator's departure from Trinidad to realize the writing ambitions nurtured with the adoption of colonial English language and culture: "So that at the moment of take-off almost, the moment of departure, the landscape of my childhood was like something which I had missed, something I had never seen" (pp. 97–98). And it is this "I," the writing "I," on which life in the symbolic order has been based, which must finally split open in order to allow an experience of origin (even if made up) to penetrate. Structurally, *The Enigma of Arrival* reinforces this notion by making "The Journey" a record of the life that results from that "miss," the life that has cut off from its past, while the true return to the images of childhood, the lost myth of origin, however fragmented, occurs in "Jack's Garden"—the record of the narrator's rebirth in Wiltshire. There, the awesome, primal symbiosis with the English landscape is punctuated with memories from Trinidad. And when that occurs, it is often even more than a tangible "working through" of the process of recouping an experience prior to language; it is the focusing on the essence of the myth-making process and its confounding combination of truth and fiction:

> I had seen the cows on the hillsides against the sky, heads down, grazing, or looking with timorous interest at the passing man. And they had seemed like the cows in the

> drawing on the label of the condensed-milk tins I knew in Trinidad as a child: something to me as a result at the very heart of romance, a child's fantasy of the beautiful, other place, something which, when I saw it on the downs, was like something I had always known (p. 80).

But at the same time as "The Journey" can be viewed as an anterior life in the symbolic order leading to disintegration and regeneration into some other, primal order, it pulls equally in the opposite direction. While the life-as-writer does begin falsely and ends in illness and breakdown, the life lived as a writer is also one of growing insight, a conscious movement towards the realization that "man and writer were the same person" (p. 102). This process evolves from denial of the past, in the hope of becoming an "English" writer, through a search for the past via the construction of history, both public and personal: "I had given myself a past, and a romance of the past. One of the loose ends in my mind had vanished; a little chasm filled" (p. 149), and ends with the acknowledgement that the internal split is irrevocable, that the past, the original myth of origin is truly lost: ". . . that my departure from my island in 1950—with all that it implied of homelessness and drift and longing—was final " (p. 152). This realization, the pulling out of the last foothold from under the narrator which precipitates his breakdown is also what makes it possible for the time in Wiltshire to be experienced and, more importantly, to be narrated later on as a birth, an origin. In other words, it is the conscious elevation of that experience to the level of a myth of origin, by a writer, writing in retrospect. For it is not only the section "The Journey" which is inserted into the happenings in Wiltshire, but the time in Wiltshire which is framed and included in the section "The Journey" as a phase, now in the past, and viewed as such by the writer: "More than ten years after I had moved to the valley, when I was almost at the end of my time there, my time in the manor cottage, my second life, I was strongly reminded of my first week in England" (p. 159). It is the writer's knowledge and exploration of himself, through writing, which has led to the naming both of his breakdown as "something like grief" (p. 94) and of his Wiltshire experience as a "second life."

Furthermore, it is the authorial devices, such as the manipulation of time, and the use of language (which will be discussed) that privilege the Wiltshire experience and position it in relation to other, past experiences. This is also true of the future. The narrator leaves the manor cottage and settles in the valley in a house that he has converted from two old cottages (one of those rare instances where life becomes a symbol for art: the narrator [Naipaul] both connects with the history of the place and reshapes it to meet his own needs). Thus although one cycle in the valley ends, another begins, and the references to the future emphasize the pastness of what is rendered in the present.

The manipulation of time extends to the connections between the sections themselves. With the exception of a few references to a time *after* the narrator's sojourn at the manor cottage, all three Wiltshire sections are concerned with the same time span, but the events described, rather than follow a chronological sequence, are grouped precisely so as to confound and disrupt our sense of time. In fact, "Jack's Garden" comprises the complete period the narrator spent at the cottage and could thus be described as a complete cycle, while "Ivy" and "Rooks" each deal, through a magnification process, with cycles within that overall narrative: cycles of English history, of Trinidadian history, and chiefly segments of the personal histories of the figures that people the manor and its surroundings. For each participant in any of these cycles, "time" is at a different stage. And this is also true of the narrator's "time" which becomes relative. Time itself thus loses not its importance, but its absoluteness, its role in charting the existence of "self" in the world. In this sense, though the sections are so much concerned with change and decay, the "dethroning" of absolute time paradoxically creates a breaking down of barriers, a wholeness before consciousness which is a kind of everlasting, primordial flux. This chaotic flux thus reinforces the primal character of the experience of absorption in the English landscape.

In addition to serving to undermine the structural absoluteness of time, the multiple cycles of *The Enigma of Arrival* also underscore the indivisibility of end from beginning. The people whom the narrator, a "witness of people and events in the valley" (p. 97), encounters, the events that pass him by, are all framed by arrivals and departures—arrivals that are ends, departures that are beginnings, and vice versa—whether temporary or permanent. Pitton the gardener, Bray's woman, Brenda and her television repair man, the Phillipses, they all depart and arrive, marry or divorce, move or die. But mostly they die: Jack and his father-in-law, Brenda, Mr Phillips, the manor itself which is a kind of microcosm of English history.

At the same time, the novel does move, through a pattern of repetition and analogy, magnification and withdrawal, almost imperceptibly in an individual cycle, the narrator's cycle: from the creation of origin to its inevitable consequence—the acquisition of self-knowledge, hence otherness and lack, and the acknowledgement and acceptance of death. "The aim of all life is death," wrote Freud.[4] To create a self, for Naipaul, is to be inserted into that cycle.

Language: Origin and Writing

I have described *The Enigma of Arrival* and particularly "Jack's Garden" as thematizing a coming into self with its opposing experiences of wholeness and loss, while at the same time being a highly contrived retrospective creation. In the passages I have chosen to discuss below, I hope to demonstrate how the use of language itself in "Jack's Garden" enacts a similar process. This may also help to explain the confusion created in one's response as a reader to this section, and to some extent to the book in general. On the one hand there is an awareness of the craftsmanship, the intellectual underpinnings of the text, and on the other, there is a sense of the text's hermeticity, a feeling that one is basically in the position of overhearing a man's recitation (both in the present and in retrospect) of his assimilation into a landscape.

The main vehicle of the double drive in the language of "Jack's Garden," the reach for the primary experience and the creation of the best rendition of it in language, is repetition.[5] And it is to this aspect of the first passage I will analyze that I chiefly wish to refer. To invoke Freud once again, in *Beyond the Pleasure Principle* there is a conflict, ultimately unresolved, between the view of the repetition compulsion as acting in the service of the ego and its drive to master and control (and in the *fort da* example to control linguistically as well as affectively), or acting in the service of a death instinct, a drive to return to a conserving, inanimate state, death, or origin. It is this very same tension that dominates the use of language in the two passages to be analyzed and which parallels the contradictory pull of seeking origin and writing about it:

> Daily I walked in the wide grassy way between the flint slopes, past chalk valleys rubbled white and looking sometimes like a Himalayan valley strewn in midsummer with old, gritted snow. Daily I saw the mounds that had been raised so many centuries before. The number of these mounds! They lay all around. From a certain height they were outlined against the sky and looked like pimples on the land. In the beginning I liked to tramp over the mounds that were more or less on my walk. The grass on these mounds was coarse; it was long-bladed, pale in colour, and grew in ankle-turning tufts or clumps. The trees, where they existed, were wind-beaten and stunted.
>
> I picked my way up and down and around each mound; I wanted in those early days to leave no accessible mound unlooked at, feeling that if I looked hard enough and long enough I might arrive, not at an understanding of the religious mystery, but an appreciation of the labour.
>
> Daily I walked in the wide grassy way—perhaps in the old days a processional way. Daily I climbed up from the bottom of the valley to the crest of the way and the view: the stone circles directly ahead, down below, but still far away: grey against green, and sometimes lit up by the sun. Going up the grassy way (and though willing to admit that the true processional path might have been elsewhere) I never ceased to imagine myself a man of those bygone times, climbing up to have this confirmation that all was well with the world (p. 23).

The activity described in the second passage is that of walking over the landscape and the beginning of relating to an Other:

> It was his father-in-law I noticed first. And it was his father-in-law I met first. I met him quite early on, while I was still exploring, and before I had settled on a regular

> daily route. I walked or picked my way down little-used lateral lanes on the hillsides, lanes deep in mud, or overgrown with tall grass, or overhung with trees. I walked in those early days along lanes or paths I was never to walk along again. And it was on one of those exploratory walks, on a lateral lane linking the steep rocky road beside the windbreak with the wider, flatter way, it was on one of those little-used, half hidden lanes that I met the father-in-law (p. 25).

The most striking linguistic feature in these passages, is, as I have indicated, repetition: of sounds (the proliferation of alliteration, assonance, half-rhyme, etc.), words, phrases, syntactic structures, and, in the first passage, the marked position of the word "Daily," giving it special prominence.

One such set of repetitions will furnish an initial example for discussion. "Daily I walked in the wide grassy way . . . Daily I saw the mounds. . . Daily I walked in the wide grassy way . . . Daily I climbed up from the bottom of the valley . . . " Here there is an obvious correlation between language and the depicted reality. The language repeats verbatim the activity it describes: the daily repetition of tramping over and exploring a particular segment of the landscape. But the relation between the language and the experience is in fact more complex. The compulsive repetitive walking over the landscape and its rendering in language can be seen at one and the same time as the repetition of the original experience, i.e., in Freud's terms the drive to return to beginnings, and thus connect up with, become one with the landscape, and the repetition in order to master and control, the function of the ego in Freud, which is already at work to ward off the loss and separation inherent in oneness.

The striving for a primal feeling through language is manifest in additional ways as well. The sameness of the phrase "Daily I," for example, implies the wish for the complete recapturing of origin without difference (whether this is possible or not). It also focuses the activity on the very basic, fundamental level—it takes little account of variety or otherness. Furthermore, in the description of his ambles, the narrator shows a propensity for using certain combinations of noun phrases, such as "the wide grassy way," "the mounds," "the lanes," "the view," repeatedly and with certain emphasis, often where one would have expected a pronoun (although pronouns do appear):

> The number of *these mounds*! They lay all around. From a certain height they were outlined against the sky and looked like pimples on the land. In the beginning I liked to tramp over *the mounds* that were more or less on my walk. The grass on *these mounds* was coarse; . . . I picked my way up and down and around *each mound*; I wanted in those early days to leave no *accessible mound* unlooked at (p. 23, my italics).

These repetitions have multiple effects. For one, they indicate a tendency towards a more concrete, and hence, in developmental terms, a more primitive level of expression. For another, they create a process of defamiliarization, a drawing attention to the sound of the word that creates a split between the apprehension of the objects and the language used. Furthermore, the repetition of the noun creates the impression of the constant rediscovery of the object perceived, a kind of perpetual reliving of the original experience.

The insistent use of the definite article in the noun phrases acts to remove us from the scene described while keeping it primarily within the narrator's experience. The narrator, we feel, has a deep knowledge of *the* way, the mounds, the view, etc., while we as readers have to be content chiefly with the general, unparticularized term or at best a superficial description. The world is filled with ways and slopes and views and even mounds of various kinds. It is the way the landscape becomes the narrator's that remains untold. The most we can gather from the narrative is that the narrator is describing something intensely *his* and not *ours*. Thus the experience remains perpetually an originating experience for the narrator, one of which we are, at best, voyeurs.

But just as the repetition discussed above brings us in tune with a kind of very primal experience, the repetition of variations of sounds and the conscious play of repetition in the craft of the language patterns, foregrounds the act of the author as originator, of ego mastery and control. For example, by divorcing sound from referent, the defamiliarization mentioned above calls our attention to the word used. In fact, the play of language in these passages is similar to that of poetry. Whether it is the alliteration: "I walked or picked my way down little-used lateral lanes on the hillsides, . . ." or the assonance and the even stronger rhyme and half-rhyme: "Lanes," "ways," "days," "lay"; or the joining of the private experience with the landscape in the words "way" (the "wider, flatter way," echoing in "I walked or picked my way"), the effect is not only of a richness of sound, but of a linking, a blanketing of sound that strives towards a wholeness, a completeness. If in the first passage this is achieved primarily by making connections between words, in the second passage, describing an early exploratory phase in becoming acquainted with the landscape, the proliferation of the repeated initial sounds, together with the repetition of words, creates a focusing and concentration, a kind of vortex into which we are drawn: "I walked in those early days along lanes or paths I was never to walk along again. And it was on one of those exploratory walks, on a lateral lane linking the steep rocky road beside the windbreak with the wider, flatter way, it was on one of those little-used, half hidden lanes," etc. Interestingly, the phrase "I was never to walk along again," while emphasizing the singularity and uniqueness of the experience on the story level, linguistically, through the use of repetition, blends past, present and future into an undifferentiated continuum.

It is interesting that the frame of the second passage is the narrator's first meeting with Jack's father-in-law. The digressive description of the circumstances, an outburst of repeated, interwoven, closely linked words, conveys the closeness and completeness of the narrator's experience in the landscape *before* he is ready to encounter the Other, the father-in-law, who is in fact only the preliminary to Jack himself.

Two additional sentences, appearing immediately before the second passage, might also serve to illustrate the way the language consciously seeks both to render and to recreate a primary, pre-language experience, while at the same time calling attention to its retrospective craftsmanship:

> So in tune with the landscape had I become, in that solitude, for the first time in England.

> Of literature and antiquity and the landscape Jack and his garden and his geese and cottage and his father-in-law seemed emanations (p. 25).

In both sentences the "normal" expectations of reading are disrupted. The neutral word order of the first sentence has been subverted and the new order creates unusual emphases: "So in tune with the landscape had I become" is not only foregrounded, thus making the creation of origin the first step, the word "so" coming at the beginning stresses the affective intensity of that experience. Furthermore, the non-neutral word order, "in tune had I become" suggests a becoming resulting from the state of being in tune rather than vice versa.

In the second sentence, the prepositional phrase ("Of literature and antiquity and the landscape") is fronted, this marked word order imitating the order of experience. Literature, antiquity and the landscape—the convergence in the narrator's experience of the symbolic order, the Name-of-the-Father and primal mother—become the source, the originator of the narrator's perception of the world in the figure of Jack and his garden and his geese, etc.

The use of language in *The Enigma of Arrival,* then, shows a shift away from the realistic, "transparent" mode with which Naipaul began his career as a novelist in the nineteenth-century English tradition and which characterizes *A House for Mr Biswas,* to a subtle exploration of the tensions between experience and language as an extension of his existential preoccupations. In the words of Peter Hughes: "Naipaul, for all the traditionalism of his early fiction, has since become in all his work a writer who does what the great Modernists do: he makes good through style what has been lost through history."[6]

Genre: A Fiction-Autobiography

The story-within-a-story, "The Enigma of Arrival," in addition to constituting a thematic *mise-en-abyme,* also provides a mirror of the relation of truth to fiction enacted in *The Enigma of Arrival* as a whole. It thus sheds important light on Naipaul's creation of a narrative mode most appropriate to *his* autobiography.

Within the continuing controversy on the definitions of autobiography, the formalist approaches to the problem have made a factual truth-intention a critical condition of the genre.[7] An autobiography is seen as the recounting of a person's life story in which the facts related, including intentional or accidental lapses, distortions, omissions etc., are extra-referential and are theoretically verifiable.

Whether or not one agrees with these definitions, or tends to obscure such boundaries by changing or expanding the notion of "truth," there can be no doubt that the consciousness of such a condition in autobiography (whether fulfilled or not) has been a potent instrument in the hands of many postmodern writers attempting to come to grips with problems of self and representation in our world. The imaginary world of novels is invaded by the author who appears as a character,[8] or the authenticity of autobiography is undermined by its declared imaginative component.[9] In Naipaul's case, the intellectual awareness and self-consciousness coincide with a crucial personal need, not only to represent self but to acquire self.

The Enigma of Arrival, I have said, constitutes Naipaul's personal experience of autobiography-writing as the creation of a myth of origin and consequently a life cycle. This *a priori* implies a fictional base in which the life narrative is grounded. It could be argued that this is no different from the predicament of any writer whose myth of origin, as I have suggested in the Introduction, may be inherited but is no less a substitute, a signifier in the chain, and hence a fiction.[10] This is indeed the case. My claim for Naipaul, however, is that colonialism did not cut him off from origin, but from a myth of origin, and that it is his recognition of his inability to make any collective myth (whether Hindu, Trinidadian—which he claims did not exist—or English) his own that has served as the basis for the autobiography that is subtitled "A Novel in Five Sections." One does not need origin for self, only the Name-of-the-Father, the transmitted symbol.

That the narrator of *The Enigma of Arrival* is Naipaul is indisputable. All the events relating to his writing career, his travels, i.e., all the biographical details up until the Wiltshire sojourn, are public knowledge. No attempt has been made to disguise places, the content of books, etc. Furthermore, the narrator of *The Enigma of Arrival* remains unnamed; only his first initial, we are told, is the same as Naipaul's. What is less verifiable is the "reality" of the experiences and mainly the characters appearing in *The Enigma of Arrival* as part of his life at the cottage. But in light of what has been said above, it is also the least important, for these are the surrounding events of a creation of a myth of origin, which ontologically cannot be anything but a fiction. *The Enigma of Arrival*, in other words, presents a "true" life grounded in a fictional base, and it is precisely this hybrid that the story "The Enigma of Arrival" and its position in the larger text represents.

The story-within-a-story is a spin-off by the narrator from two interpretative acts: a painting and its entitlement by a poet. The story is first conceived by the narrator shortly after his arrival in Wiltshire, as an escape, it would seem, from the arduous labour of writing a book on Africa (*In a Free State*), and is only recognized much later to be "an idea that came innocently, without the writer suspecting how much of his life, how many aspects of his life, that remote story (still just an idea for a story) carried" (p. 96).

The original painting remains the same, but "it changed in my memory. The original (or the reproduction in the 'Little Library of Art' booklet) was always a surprise" (p. 91). And indeed in *The Enigma of Arrival* itself there are at least two versions of the imagined story, one given at the beginning of the section, the other at the end. But the story is said not only to be a version of the narrator's life, i.e., a story reflecting a fictional reality (which we know to correspond with reality), but a version of the book the narrator is writing, i.e., by implication, a "truth" reflecting a fiction. It is also important to remember that the original scene is itself a painting, a figment of Chirico's imagination, or at most an interpretation of reality. Thus the scene of "The Enigma of Arrival" functions as a kind of primal scene, at once origin of narrative and a fictional construct, which, representing the life prior to the rebirth in Wiltshire is, in fact, a myth of origin. Like the contemporary psychoanalyst who seeks to help the patient reconstruct a life narrative, whether fantasized or not, rather than dig up the elusive or non-existent original repressed, which was the goal of classical psychoanalysis, Naipaul has resolved his lack of cultural "primal scene" by consciously creating one and using it as a point of departure for a narrative which *is* a true life story whose basic fictionality is acknowledged in structure and in declaration.[11]

The story-within-the-story, however, like *The Enigma of Arrival* itself, complicates this basic relation, rendering the question of truth and fictionality in autobiography a series of positions ricocheting one off the other to create an indivisible texture. For the story, the narrator tells us, reflects his own, which we know to be Naipaul's own, story and thus confirms it, gives it shape and meaning. But the story, a fictional construct, is itself based on a fiction, which, by giving rise to many possible stories, loses its absoluteness. The story is first conceived precisely at the time when the narrator is experiencing a sense of identification with the landscape which he later, in retrospect, will shape into a narrative of origin, just as he recognizes the painting's allegorical qualities for himself only later. The painting thus reflects "reality" which is given meaning by a fiction.

It is an uncanny coincidence that while the book was going to press, the author's brother, Shiva Naipaul, to whom the book is dedicated, died suddenly. The framing of the book by two real deaths, that of the sister, set in a fictional mode, and that of the brother representing fact, poignantly reflects the ironies of the book's preoccupation with truth and fiction.

Conclusion

Simon During, in his article "Postmodernism or Post-colonialism?" at one point asks: ". . . might it not be that a single work may be postmodern in the light of one set of interests and values and postcolonialist in the light of another?"[1] In the preceding pages I have traced Naipaul's development as a writer in search of self. In so doing I have suggested that this quest has been successful and that it has taken the form of the creation of an unusual autobiography, *The Enigma of Arrival*.[2] While Naipaul's solution to his predicament is uniquely his, and it is primarily with that healing project that this study has been concerned, the Lacanian scheme outlined in the Introduction would indicate that the formative conditions of the conflict can be universalized. And, without entering into the ideological debate fuelled by Naipaul's intellectual attitudes, I have indirectly claimed that as a self-builder he is no less a post-colonial than many of his peers and critics who would deny him that collective appellation.

The Enigma of Arrival, however, besides constituting Naipaul's definitive autobiography, also contains what I would call postmodern elements, especially with regards to its blurring of the distinction between literary genres through its manipulation of truth/fiction relations. Thus, although the relationship between the postmodern and the post-colonial is not, strictly speaking, within the scope of this book, I would like to use this traditional summing-up space to discuss, however briefly, the light Naipaul's particular writing life sheds on the problem.

A large proportion of recent post-colonial criticism and theory is taken up with defining, judging or denying the links between postmodernism and post-colonialism in literature. The manifest use of similar themes and formal strategies in both camps would seem to be at odds with the antithetical philosophies or aims that inform them both. Postmodernism's rejection of the authority of "The—primarily historical—master narratives," in the words of During,[3] to confer order and meaning on the present runs counter to the need in post-colonial literature not only to rewrite colonial history but to historicize as a basis for the creation of an identity. The process of decentering and fragmentation which characterizes postmodern thought is the enemy of post-colonial nations which are busy trying to gather the remains of their repressed, forgotten, abused indigenous cultures into an entity with a centre which will hold. The same is true of postmodernism's existential "challenges to the coherent, autonomous subject,"[4] which are in contrast to the post-colonial authors' more ideologically motivated drive to recreate self, a "need for an identity granted not in terms of the colonial power, but in terms of themselves."[5] And finally, postmodernism and post-colonialism are on opposite sides with regards to the self/other binary relation. If postmodernism is "that thought which refuses to turn the Other into the Same. . . ." thus granting the Other its space of existence,[6] it also continues to operate "as a Euro-American hegemony, whose global appropriation of time-and-place inevitably proscribes certain cultures as backwards and marginal while co-opting to itself certain of their cultural 'raw' materials."[7] Post-colonialism, on the other hand, *is* that Other, and sees its task as preserving its integrity at least partially through resistance to postmodernism's globalizing tendency.

Yet that such natural adversaries as postmodernist and post-colonialist writers should use similar literary means of expression is not all that surprising. Without attempting to grapple here with the formal antecedents and developments of either, some channels of interaction seem indisputable. On the one hand, formal strategies developed regionally, such as magic realism, have been appropriated as a postmodern tool of trade. On the other, post-colonial writers who are regarded as postmodernists by some have been the recipients, by and large, of a Western education and many have chosen to live in the West where they have influenced and are influenced by current intellectual trends. Moreover, however ideologically distasteful, the imported colonial language with its attendant cultural baggage, in the absence of a viable alternative, became the symbolic order from within which most post-colonial writers address their struggle for identity.

The surveyors of this overlap differ in their assessment of it. Views range from those who equate postmodernism and post-colonialism to those who regard them as antithetical. A growing consensus seems to be that "A number of strategies, such as the move away from realist representation, the refusal of closure, the exposure of the politics of metaphor, the interrogation of forms . . . are characteristic of both the generally post-colonial and the European postmodern—but they are energised by different theoretical assumptions and by vastly different political motivations."[8] Whereas the postmodern techniques arise from postmodernism's universalist questioning and deconstruction of accepted, particularly humanist, tenets, the post-colonial predilection for formal characteristics such as irony and parody is seen variously as subverting imperialist discourse from within and resisting appropriation, and its emphasis on the local, the historicized and the referential is regarded as a way not only to oppose the forces of postmodernism but to reconstruct an identity and reclaim local history.

Unlike other post-colonial writers whose designation as postmodern or post-colonial must be formulated chiefly on ideological grounds, Naipaul's split between his intellectual allegiance and his self-building project offers a particularly interesting example of the ways the postmodern and the post-colonial can unite rather than be at odds.

In the case I have made for Naipaul as a post-colonial I have naturally stressed his rejection of the given traditions of English literature in the process of finding the appropriate expression for his particular brand of selfhood. *The Enigma of Arrival*, however, in addition to enacting the creation of that self through the creation of a myth of origin, also demonstrates how much Naipaul owes to the intellectual climate in which he has spent the past thirty years or more.

Naipaul's blurring of the boundaries between fiction and non-fiction or between the novel and autobiography in *The Enigma of Arrival* is more than the conflation of two literary modes, a practice going back centuries, where, as in the case of tragicomedy, the two components are essentially fictional. In its manipulation of genre relations *The Enigma of Arrival* engages with at least two postmodern preoccupations: the problem of referentiality, and the status of history.

Writers of traditional autobiographies, even when acknowledging the impossibility of rendering the absolute and whole truth about oneself, did base their endeavour on what could be called a truth intention, which presupposed both that it is possible to distinguish between what is or was, and what isn't or wasn't, and that history exists and can be narrativized. They further assumed, along with writers in other modes, that works based on the imagination and those founded on facts stood in a different relation to the real world, and that there was a causal relation between the past and the present.

Postmodern thought, on the other hand, has called into question most if not all of those assumptions. The "culture of simulacrum"[9] has done away with a central point of reference in the world thus blurring the distinction between that which "records" it and that which recreates or imitates it. The linearity of history and its implication in the present has been overthrown, and the possibility of forging self beyond its inscription in language has been questioned. These negations, however, besides calling into question genre boundaries such as those between autobiography and fiction, have also, paradoxically, "freed" both fiction and autobiography from traditional restrictions. The slippage between the imagined and the real has allowed for bold crossings over and mingling—between fiction and autobiography, and between history and fiction. The self is recognized as a construct historical gaps can be filled with as much authority by the imagination as by the scholarly unearthing of documents.

There is no doubt that Naipaul's alliance with the West, his adoption of the usurper father's culture, has provided him with the intellectual understanding of the mythical construct of self, as well as with the tools to take advantage of alternatives to traditional modes of self expression (even though thereby reenacting postmodernism's predicament of being trapped within its own terms of discourse). *The Enigma of Arrival* creates referential uncertainty by using verifiable biographical information in a work subtitled "A Novel." To this it adds elements of the postmodernist refusal of closure by disrupting linearity of narrative and chronology, by conflating past, present and future, by the employment of both repetition and gaps and by recycling beginnings into ends and ends into beginnings. This self-conscious engagement with and manipulation of textual materials and modes, besides indicating a break with traditional renderings of life histories, emphasizes the myth-making, constructive components of the experience of self as well as its linguistic basis.

At the same time, the pull of the underside of Naipaul's writing life, the quest for a personal history grounded in a larger cultural heritage which is the post-colonial project, has led him to seek a way of historicizing and creating a reference point outside himself as a beginning. The creation of his own myth of origin in a uniquely executed autobiographical mode has been his way of harnessing the postmodern to the post-colonial. While this overriding conceptual framework probably precludes *The Enigma of Arrival* from being a true postmodern work, it does act as an edifice which both parts of Naipaul's personality can inhabit.

Notes

Introduction

1. The term 'self' is used frequently and freely in studies on Naipaul to denote a wide range of concepts, such as identity, self-definition, biography and history. My use of the term, while containing echoes of all those perspectives, is drawn from the psychoanalytic, particularly the Lacanian, view of subject, with added dimensions, as shall be elaborated upon further.

2. For the sake of clarity and convenience, in my use of the terms post-colonial and postmodern I am adopting Helen Tiffin's delimitation of the post-colonial as that which "has been used to describe writing and reading practices grounded in some form of colonial experiences occurring outside Europe but as a consequence of European expansion into and exploitation of 'other worlds'," and her equation of the postmodern and post-structuralist to include "Euro-American theories that take issue, in a number of ways, with the precepts of Saussurian linguistic structuralism" ("Post-Colonialism, Post-Modernism and the Rehabilitation of Post-Colonial History," *Journal of Commonwealth Literature*, 23:1 [1988]: 169–181).

3. The following summary of Lacan's position is based on: Jacques Lacan, *Ecrits: A Selection*, trans. Alan Sheridan (London: Tavistock Publications, 1977), especially the sections: "On the possible treatment of psychosis," pp. 192–99, and "Function and field of speech and language," pp. 65–73; Anika Lemaire, *Jacques Lacan*, trans. David Macey (London: Routledge & Kegan Paul, 1977), pp. 83–90; J. Laplanche & J-B. Pontalis, *The Language of Psychoanalysis*, trans. Donald Nicholson-Smith, with an Introduction by Daniel Lagache (London: The Hogarth Press, 1985), pp. 210, 282–287, 439–441; Elizabeth Wright, *Psychoanalytic Criticism* (London & New York: Methuen, 1984), pp. 107–113.

4. I am using the term "pre-verbal world" in its broadest possible application, to include both Lacan's Imaginary and the various object relation theories which concentrate on the infant's primal tie with the mother. I am thus intentionally avoiding the issue of the ultimate existence of origin. For the purpose of my metaphoric use of the Lacanian construct, it is sufficient that to be a subject necessarily involves the inaccessibility of origin.

5. Jacques Derrida, "Structure, Sign and Play in the Discourse of the Human Sciences," in *Writing and Difference*, trans. Alan Bass (London: Routledge & Kegan Paul, 1978), p. 280.

6. Ibid.

7. Selwyn R. Cudjoe, whose *V. S. Naipaul, A Materialist Reading* (Amherst, Mass: The University of Massachusetts Press, 1988) touches on my study at many points, proposes a somewhat different psychoanalytic structure to describe the transition from the colonial to the post-colonial, or from "a position of non-identity to a definable identity" (p. 102). The colonial (individual or society) is in a state of undifferentiated narcissistic identification with the mother country, which for Cudjoe is the source country of the colonizing power, in this case England. To become a post-colonial subject, the individual (society) must emerge through the mirror stage into the symbolic order to achieve a separate identity. Naipaul, however, succeeded in this only partially: "Naipaul's desire to understand the colonial subject and the manner in which she or he functions in the social totality pushes him further toward a historical explanation, but his inability to move fully out of the mirror stage of development and assume a social identity separate and distinct from that of the mother (country) results in his feelings of fragmentation and loss, disorder and helplessness, isolation and unease. Until he can remove himself from his incestuous relationship with the mother (country), he cannot articulate an autonomous subject or comprehensively understand how that subject functions in the era of independence" (p. 111). If Cudjoe accepts this basic structure as being the case, making the colonial mother country the "motherland" for the colonial subject paradoxically serves as a confirmation of Naipaul's experience of Trinidadian culture as non-existent, as it does away with the possibility of a past prior to the colonial "parenthood."

8. Janet Gunn, *Autobiography: Toward a Poetics of Experience* (Philadelphia: University of Pennsylvania Press, 1982), pp. 3–10.

9. Argued and postulated in various writings; see, for example, Michel Foucault, "What is an Author?" in *Textual Strategies: Perspectives in Post-Structuralist Criticism*, ed. and trans. Josue V. Harari (London:

Methuen, 1979), pp. 141–160; Paul de Man, "Autobiography as Defacement," in *The Rhetoric of Romanticism* (New York: Columbia University Press, 1984), pp. 67–81; Roland Barthes, "The Death of the Author," in *Image-Music-Text*, translated and edited by Stephen Heath (London: Fontana, 1979).

10. *Finding the Centre* (London: Penguin Books, 1984), p. 87. Henceforth all citations from this work are from this edition, and will be given parenthetically in the text.

11. V. S. Naipaul, *The Overcrowded Barracoon* (London: Penguin Books, 1972), p. 24. All citations from this work are from this edition and are given parenthetically in the text.

12. Especially in interviews and essays. See, for example, interview with Ian Hamilton, "Without a Place": "At the back of my mind the thing that embarrasses me slightly about my very early work is that because of my assumptions about the nature of the world I really thought I was writing about a world that was fairly whole. It took me a long time to see that I had no society to write about." Reprinted in *Critical Perspectives on V. S. Naipaul*, ed. Robert D. Hamner (London: Heinemann, 1979), pp. 39–47.

13. The relationship of Naipaul's writing to that of his father, Seepersad Naipaul, is a complex one. Not only was Naipaul instrumental in bringing out the posthumous publication of his father's stories in England, under the title *The Adventures of Gurudeva and Other Stories* (London: Andre Deutsch, 1976), but he incorporated parts of them in his own work (see n. 19 in my chapter on *A House for Mr Biswas*). According to Anthony Boxill ("V. S. Naipaul's Starting Point," *Journal of Commonwealth Literature* 10 [August 1975]: 3–5), his father's stories provided Naipaul with an example of how his reality could be rendered into writing. Whereas Landeg White (*V. S. Naipaul, A Critical Introduction* (London: Macmillan, 1975) has pointed out that Naipaul's father's stories were a two-fold source: a) of a way to fictionalize Trinidad and source material, and b) of the motif of escape which he (Naipaul) fulfilled.

14. There is an interesting complication and reversal here of Otto Rank's theory (repeated in Freud's "Family Romances," *Standard Edition of the Complete Psychological Works of Sigmund Freud*. Trans. and ed. James Strachey. 24 Vols. [London: The Hogarth Press, 1953–74], 9, pp. 237–241) of the myth of the birth of the hero. In *The Myth of the Birth of the Hero and Other Writings* (New York: Vintage Press, 1959), Rank psychoanalytically analyzes and categorizes the universal ways the births (i.e., origins) of heroes are mythologized in collective mythologies. In Naipaul's biography, the non-hero (who lacks a

collective to mythologize him) must create his own mythology which, through denial, becomes a myth of non-origin.

15. In an interview with Ronald Bryden (*The Listener*, 22 March 1973, pp. 367–370), Naipaul outlined two main reasons for moving away from fiction to non-fiction. The first was that he could not reconcile his education with his background in writing: "I feel that the simple society cannot lend itself to extended imaginative treatment." And secondly, fiction, as a universalized experience, could not serve as the vehicle for his personal experience: "It's something that cannot be converted into fiction. It is almost too private."

16. Peter Hughes, *V. S. Naipaul* (London & New York: Routledge, 1988), p. 29.

17. That is, language used as a means of action in certain contexts and with certain intentions, as formulated by Elizabeth Bruss, in *Autobiographical Acts, The Changing Situation of a Literary Genre* (Baltimore and London: The Johns Hopkins University Press, 1976). This topic is elaborated upon further in chapter 2.

18. The three books Naipaul has written since *The Enigma of Arrival*: *A Turn in the South* (New York: Alfred Knopf, 1989), *India: A Million Mutinies Now* (London: Heinemann, 1990), and *A Way in the World* (New York: Alfred Knopf, 1994), constitute a further resolution of his conflictual relations with his past.

19. Especially among Caribbean writers such as George Lamming (*The Pleasures of Exile* [London: Michael Joseph, 1960]), who view Naipaul's position as a denial of the nascent culture and literature of the region. For one of many references to this issue, see: John Thieme, "V. S. Naipaul's Third World: A Not So Free State," *Journal of Commonwealth Literature* 10 (August 1975): 10–22.

20. At the same time I do not believe that my work falls into the category of what Cudjoe calls "idealist" interpretations: readings that "seek to reproduce and to reemphasize the self-evident truth of Naipaul's judgments and the brilliance of his observation" (*V. S. Naipaul, A Materialist Reading*, p. 4). On the contrary, I offer my psychoanalytic concept as a structure upon which any number of readings, materialist as well as ideological, can find a place. For example, Patrick Parrinder, in his article, "V. S. Naipaul and the Uses of Literacy," *Critical Quarterly* 21 (Summer 1979): 5–13, translates what I have called "life in the symbolic order" into an examination of the power of literacy in the post-colonial world. According to him, Naipaul's literacy, i.e., his adoption of the literary tradition of England and the West allowed him "the freedom to write and partake of the

literary spirit," but for his characters "its meaning is always problematic, since literacy comes to them not as a natural inheritance but as an aspect of the 'synthetic' cultures of the post-Imperial world" (p. 6).

21. Abdul R. JanMohamed, "The Economy of Manichean Allegory: The Function of Racial Difference in Colonialist Literature," in *"Race," Writing and Difference*, ed. Henry Louis Gates, Jr. (Chicago & London: The University of Chicago Press, 1985), pp. 78–106. See also Edward Said's comments on Naipaul in "Intellectuals in the Post-Colonial World," *Salmagundi* 70–71 (1986): 80–81.

22. Rob Nixon, *London Calling, V. S. Naipaul, Postcolonial Mandarin*, (New York, Oxford: Oxford University Press, 1992), p. 14.

23. In *The Forms of Autobiography* (New Haven: Yale University Press, 1980), and "Autobiography and the Cultural Moment: A Thematic, Historical, and Bibliographical Introduction," in *Autobiography, Essays Theoretical and Critical*, ed. James Olney (Princeton: Princeton University Press, 1980), respectively.

24. Including, among others: Georges Gusdorf, "Conditions and Limits of Autobiography," in *Autobiography, Essays Theoretical and Critical*, pp. 28–48, who was one of the first to posit the self as a product of a cultural concept; Roy Pascal, *Design and Truth in Autobiography* (Cambridge, Mass.: Harvard University Press, 1960); Francis Hart, "Notes for an Anatomy of Modern Autobiography," *New Literary History* 1 (1970): 485–511; and Philippe Lejeune, "The Autobiographical Contract," in *French Literary Theory Today*, ed. Tzvetan Todorov, trans. R. Carter (Cambridge, England: Cambridge University Press, 1982), pp. 192–222.

25. For example, Spengemann, *The Forms of Autobiography*; Janet Gunn, *Autobiography: Toward a Poetics of Experience*; Paul Jay, *Being in the Text: Self-Representation from Wordsworth to Roland Barthes* (Ithaca: Cornell University Press, 1984); Avrom Fleishman, *Figures of Autobiography* (Berkeley: University of California Press, 1983), and others. I would also include in this group the deconstruction of self and autobiography, at the most extreme pole of which is Paul de Man in "Autobiography as Defacement."

26. Peter Abbott, "Autobiography, Autography, Fiction: Groundwork for a Taxonomy of Textual Categories," *New Literary History* 19 (Spring 1988): p. 600.

27. Ibid., 609.

28. Paul Jay, for example, calls it "The Art of Fictional Representation" (*Being in the Text*, p. 115).

29. Princeton: Princeton University Press, 1985.

30. Ibid., p. 4.

31. Ibid., p. 5.

32. Ibid., pp. 3, 5–6.

Chapter One: *A House for Mr Biswas*

1. Spengemann, *The Forms of Autobiography*, p. xiii.

2. First published by Andre Deutsch, 1961. All page references are from the Penguin Books (London, 1969) edition, and are given parenthetically in the text.

3. I am aware of the seeming fallacy of viewing Naipaul's entire oeuvre through the perspective of autobiography which is a Western concept, while attempting to account also for what is outside of Western experience. While it is true that my study does not explore the symbolic repetition of the lost Hindu heritage as it is enacted in the life of Mr Biswas, and for that matter in the life of Naipaul himself, I would say that it is precisely the attempt to forge an identity through the delimiting, excluding parameters of Western culture and denying the other heritage with which this study is concerned.

4. The first three have been aptly described by Michael Thorpe (in *V. S. Naipaul* [Harlow, Essex: Longman Group Ltd, 1976], p. 9) as "comedies of Trinidadian manners."

5. Spengemann, *The Forms of Autobiography*, p. 132.

6. See White, *V. S. Naipaul, A Critical Introduction*, especially chap. 4; Boxill, "V. S. Naipaul's Starting Point," p. 109; and Hughes, *V. S. Naipaul*, pp. 39–40. My reading of *A House for Mr Biswas*, as well as my view of Naipaul's entire early period, has a strong affinity with the respective chapters in White's *V. S. Naipaul, A Critical Introduction*.

7. Gordon Rohler, "Character and Rebellion in *A House for Mr Biswas*," in *Critical Perspectives on V. S. Naipaul*, ed. Robert D. Hamner.

8. Thorpe, *V. S. Naipaul*, p. 15.

9. John Thieme, "Ralph Singh's Journey in *The Mimic Men*," *Modern Fiction Studies* 30 (Autumn 1984): 509. See also Cudjoe, *V. S. Naipaul, A Materialist Reading*, pp. 51–52.

10. Ibid., p. 12: "The conflict in Naipaul's writing involves the clash between Eastern and Western perceptions of the world."

11. Sigmund Freud, "The Ego and the Superego," *Standard Edition,* 19 (1961), pp. 28–39; "The Dissolution of the Oedipus Complex," *Standard Edition,* 19 (1961), pp. 173–179.

12. Lemaire, *Jacques Lacan,* p. 83.

13. Sigmund Freud, *Totem and Taboo, Standard Edition,* 13 (1955), pp. 140–146.

14. See also Lacan, *Ecrits,* pp. 22–24.

15. Lemaire, *Jacques Lacan,* p. 85.

16. Ibid.

17. Ibid., p. 90.

18. Ibid., p. 83.

19. Laplanche & Pontalis, *The Language of Psychoanalysis,* pp. 211–212. The autobiographical import of this incorporation finds no more remarkable expression than in Naipaul's use of parts of stories written by his father in his own work, especially in *A House for Mr Biswas.* For a detailed examination of this phenomenon, see John Thieme, *The Web of Tradition* (Hertfordshire, England: Dangaroo Press/ Hansib Publications, 1987), pp. 57–64.

20. The subject of women in the writings of V. S. Naipaul is a complex one and beyond the scope of this study. Briefly, as a displacement of the mother "taken over" by the usurper colonial father, women tend to appear either as idealized victims, as in the above example, or as collaborators—castrating, manipulative, etc. For an illuminating discussion of the role of women in Naipaul's writings, see, for example, Robert Hemenway, "Sex and Politics in V. S. Naipaul," *Studies in the Novel* 14 (Summer 1982): 189–202.

21. Naipaul's subsequent writing of *The Loss of El Dorado* was an attempt to rectify this situation by writing a personalized account of Raleigh's experiences in the region.

22. Sigmund Freud, *The Interpretation of Dreams, Standard Edition,* 4 (1953), pp. 225–226.

23. Gaston Bachelard, *The Poetics of Space* (Boston: Beacon Press, 1979), pp. 4–8.

24. The striving of all living things to return to an inanimate state: Sigmund Freud, *Beyond the Pleasure Principle, Standard Edition,* 18 (1955), p. 38.

25. It is not accidental that the second half of the novel is set in Port of Spain as opposed to the rural areas. As many critics have noted, Mr Biswas's personal transition from his non-existence in the world of

the Tulsis into a life in the word as a journalist in Port of Spain is repeated at the level of the family, in the disintegration of the Tulsi clan and its gradual move to Port of Spain and into Western mores, and of the Indian segment of the society as a whole. See for example, R. H. Lee, "The Novels of V. S. Naipaul," in *Critical Perspectives on V. S. Naipaul*, ed. Robert D. Hamner, pp. 74–78; Maureen Warner-Lewis, "Cultural Confrontation, Disintegration and Syncretism in 'A House for Mr Biswas'," ibid., pp. 98–100; and Thieme, *The Web of Tradition*, pp. 82–83.

26. A similar outlook on Mr Biswas's progress through writing is outlined in Cudjoe, *V. S. Naipaul, A Materialist Reading*, pp. 60–62.

Chapter Two: *The Overcrowded Barracoon*

1. V. S. Naipaul, *The Overcrowded Barracoon* (London: Penguin Books, 1976). All page references are from this edition, and are given parenthetically in the text.

2. *The Middle Passage* (1962), *The Loss of El Dorado* (1969), *An Area of Darkness* (1964), and *India: A Wounded Civilization* (1977), among others.

3. As discussed, for example, in *The Return of Eva Peron* (London: Penguin Books, 1981), pp. 217–218, and in an interview with Ronald Bryden, *The Listener*, 29 March 1973, pp. 367–370.

4. In *Autobiographical Acts*.

5. (London: Penguin Books, 1973). This novel was Naipaul's only attempt to write about English society from within.

6. Landeg White describes the first two phases of Naipaul's writing career as follows: "For if *A House for Mr Biswas* is the climax of the first phase of Naipaul's career, a phase in which he writes almost exclusively about the society he has escaped, *The Mimic Men* clearly marks the end of the second phase, the end of an absorption with his personal homelessness. . . ." (*V. S. Naipaul: A Critical Introduction*, p. 10).

7. As elaborated by Naipaul himself in various instances. See *A Middle Passage* (London: Penguin Books, 1969), pp. 56–58. For other treatments of the subject, see, for example, *The Islands in Between*, ed. Louis James (London: Oxford University Press, 1968), pp. 1–6.

8. In *Finding the Centre* (1984). See n. 18 in my chapter on *A House for Mr Biswas*.

9 This is apparent in both of his book-length studies of India of this period: *An Area of Darkness* and *India: A Wounded Civilization* (1977).

10. Lacan, *Ecrits*, pp. 192–199. See also Lemaire, *Jacques Lacan*, pp. 173–175.

11. A definitive description of Naipaul's inability to see outside the symbolic order of the West is given by Cudjoe: "It never occurs to Naipaul that he could explore Indian writing (be it the novel or the autobiography) from within its own indigenous boundaries, its own mode of looking at itself. . . . Because Naipaul treats the Western experience as the universal experience, a final closure of all knowledge and the beginning and end of all history, even that which is to come, he cannot perceive, nor would he allow himself to believe, that the Western experience, like the African or Indian, was only a partial experience of the social totality called world" (*V. S. Naipaul, A Materialist Reading*, pp. 130–131).

12. O. Mannoni, *Prospero and Caliban* (New York: Frederick A. Praeger, 1964), pp. 97–109.

13. Ibid., pp. 110–112.

14. The publication of *Foe* by J. M. Coetzee has given rise to numerous illuminating discussions on the postmodern, post-colonial issue. See, for example, Richard Begam, "Silence and Mut(e)ilation: White Writing in J. M. Coetzee's *Foe*," *South Atlantic Quarterly* 93:1 (Winter 1994): 111-129 and Sheila Roberts, "Post-colonialism, or the House of Friday—J. M. Coetzee's *Foe*," *World Literature Written in English* 31:1 (Spring 1991): 87–92.

15. *V. S. Naipaul*, p. 62.

16. *The Loss of El Dorado*, p. 13.

17. Themes which form the core of Naipaul's confrontation with the Trinidad of his past in *The Middle Passage*.

18 *Autobiographical Acts*, p. 2.

19. Ibid., p. 5.

20. Ibid.

21. Ibid., p. 10.

22. Ibid., pp. 10–11.

23. Ibid.

24. Ibid., p. 12

Chapter Three: *In a Free State*

1. London: Penguin Books, 1973. All page references are from this edition and are given parenthetically in the text.

2. See, for example, Robert Hamner, "Character and Setting," in *Critical Perspectives on V. S. Naipaul*: ". . . they [Ralph Singh and Bobby] exemplify the decadence and emptiness consequent upon living inauthentically in a world which, for no discernible reason, has come to appear devoid of meaning" (p. 233).

3. See, for example, Kerry McSweeney, "V. S. Naipaul: Sensibility and Schemata," *Critical Quarterly* 18 (Autumn 1976): 73–79; and Linda Anderson, "Ideas of Identity and Freedom in V. S. Naipaul and Joseph Conrad," *English Studies* 59 (December 1978): 515.

4. White, *V. S. Naipaul, A Critical Introduction*, p. 195.

5. Anderson, "Ideas of Identity and Freedom in V. S. Naipaul and Joseph Conrad," p. 515.

6 It is interesting at this point to compare Robert Morris's view that the characters in *In a Free State* exist in the illusion that "to be in continual exile is somehow to be continually free" (*Paradoxes of Order*, pp. 74–75) with the view that Cudjoe develops. Cudjoe sees *In a Free State* as an example of Naipaul's last phase of writing, in which, due to his personal distancing from Trinidad, he tended "to render his society in a naturalistic manner and [this] prevented him from capturing the psychic trauma and emotional development experienced by the newly freed subjects or recognizing the human psyche as a specific social entity that is reorganized and reconstituted into a more specific unity in historical time" (*V. S. Naipaul, A Materialist Reading*, p. 141).

7. See Mannoni, *Prospero and Caliban*, pp. 110–112.

8. Anderson, "Ideas of Identity and Freedom in V. S. Naipaul and Joseph Conrad," p. 515.

9. It is interesting to compare this description with the descriptions of Wiltshire in *The Enigma of Arrival*, where the merging into the landscape is successful (see Chapter five).

10. See Chapter One, on *A House for Mr Biswas*. For an interesting critique of Freud's theory, see Larry David Nachman, "Psychoanalysis and Social Theory: The Origin of Society and of Guilt," *Salmagundi* 52–53 (Spring–Summer 1981): 65–106.

11. See, for example, Morris in *Paradoxes of Order*: ". . . And while it is true that Naipaul has elsewhere shown a detachment when writing

autobiography as severe as when writing fiction, the 'facts' of *In a Free State* cannot help but lend greater truth and conviction to its 'fancy'" (p. 74).

12. White, *V. S. Naipaul, A Critical Introduction*, p. 207.

13. *Paradoxes of Order*, p. 74.

Chapter Four: *Finding the Centre*

1. London: Penguin Books, 1984. All page references to this work are from this edition, and are given parenthetically in the text.

2. Peter Hughes has written in a similar vein: "This double pull toward and away from, a reciprocal and mythic translation between the imaginative life and the history of peoples, explains the interplay between fictions and histories throughout his [Naipaul's] writing life" (*V. S. Naipaul*, p. 84).

3. For an analogous reading of the relation of *Finding the Centre* to *The Enigma of Arrival*, see Cudjoe, *V. S. Naipaul, A Materialist Reading*, pp. 210–211. But whereas in my analysis self knowledge is a key to resolution, for Cudjoe the confrontation with the past will lead only to the ultimate delusion. See the chapter on *The Enigma of Arrival*.

4. Collected in *Miguel Street* (London: Andre Deutsch, 1959).

5. In Lacan's mirror stage, the infant first forms his illusionary sense of self by seeing his image in the mirror. See *Ecrits*, pp. 1–7.

6. In Chapter One, p. 22.

7. *V. S. Naipaul*, p. 27.

8. And in *A Bend in the River* (London: Penguin Books, 1980).

9. That Mr Biswas's sensitive stomach was derived from his father's indigestion problems is described more than once. See "Prologue to an Autobiography," p. 35. Naipaul's own fastidiousness concerning food, no doubt connected to his Hindu background, is described in various writings. See, for example, *The Overcrowded Barracoon*, pp. 33–35.

10. A direction indicated already in *In a Free State*. This is not to say that he was at this point no longer to write fiction, only that in those writings in which the drive towards autobiography is the main goal, an alternative to fiction was being sought. See Hughes, *V. S. Naipaul*, p. 29.

11. Both Hughes (*V. S. Naipaul*, pp. 103–104) and White have commented on the quality of Naipaul's imagination. As early as 1975 White wrote: "Naipaul is a novelist not a reporter. But it is fair to suggest that on the whole his is a shaping rather than an inventive imagination" (*V. S. Naipaul, A Critical Introduction*, p. 24). Whereas Robert Hemenway describes Naipaul's position vis-a-vis the imagination as an idealism "arising from the author's confidence, some might say arrogance, in the artist's talent for seeing clearly, for puncturing illusions. . . . Naipaul elevates the act of perceiving, the process of observing what 'really' is, to the status of religious ritual, an artistic act of faith" ("Sex and Politics in V. S. Naipaul," p. 191).

Chapter Five: *The Enigma of Arrival*

1. London: Viking, 1987. All page references to this work are from this edition, and are given parenthetically in the text.

2. Selwyn Cudjoe (*V. S. Naipaul, A Materialist Reading*, p. 215), has called Naipaul's response to the landscape in *The Enigma of Arrival* "a fantasy of origins," based on Laplanche and Pontalis's writings on the origins of sexuality. The process he observes is similar to the one I am suggesting: "Thus, the text is not so much an autobiography of his socio-cultural life, as it is a linguistic unfolding of a consciousness, an attachment to a new land and the evolution of a new sensibility" (p. 212). But his conclusions are radically different. Rather than the resolution of conflict, Cudjoe sees *The Enigma of Arrival* as "the most intense of all his fantasies," leading, by his "unconscious desire to thrust Trinidad out of his mind" (p. 216), to hysterical conversion and a splitting of consciousness. The gap stems, I think, in large part from our different vantage points. While my study of Naipaul attempts to read his writings as a revelation of a subjective experience, without regard to how that experience is received, Cudjoe's project is diagnostic, an attempt to place Naipaul within the larger historical-cultural context.

3. *Beyond the Pleasure Principle, Standard Edition*, 18 (1955), p. 44.

4. Ibid., p. 38.

5. See Hughes, *V. S. Naipaul*, pp. 19, 21.

6. Ibid., p. 19. Landeg White, in discussing Naipaul's struggles to find an appropriate form to integrate his Hindu background and his Western assumptions, writes: "Naipaul's first books, then, are not only attempts to give a coherent picture of the society he has escaped. They

are also attempts to clarify the assumptions inherent in the form he is using. . ." (*V. S. Naipaul, A Critical Introduction*, p. 16).

7. This is true both for Elizabeth Bruss and Philippe Lejeune.

8. As in Paul Auster, *The New York Trilogy* (London: Faber & Faber, 1988) and in the works of writers such as Martin Amis and Philip Roth.

9. From Andre Malraux's *Antimemoirs*, trans. Terence Kilmartin (London: Penguin Books, 1970) and Mary McCarthy's *Memories of a Catholic Girlhood* (New York: Harcourt, 1957), to Nabokov's *Speak Memory* (London: Penguin Books, 1969).

10. The equation I am making here between substitute and fiction applies only insofar as a myth of origin is a creation which comes to substitute for origin.

11. See, for example, Donald Spence, *Narrative Truth and Historical Truth: Meaning and Interpretation in Psychoanalysis* (New York: Norton, 1982); Roy Schafer, *The Analytic Attitude* (New York: Basic Books, 1983); Peter Brooks, "The Idea of Psychoanalytic Literary Criticism," in *Discourse in Literature and Psychoanalysis*, ed. Shlomith Rimmon-Kenan (London: Methuen, 1987).

Conclusion

1. Simon During, "Postmodernism or Post-colonialism?" *Landfall* 39:3 (1985): p. 372.

2. Naipaul's three subsequent books after *The Enigma of Arrival*, *A Turn in the South*, *India: A Million Mutinies Now*, and *A Way in the World*, are books of reconciliation that could not have been written without that successful resolution.

3. Simon During, "Postmodernism or Post-colonialism?" p. 367.

4. Linda Hutcheon, "Circling the Downspout of Empire," in *Past the Last Post*, eds. I. Adam and H. Tiffin (New York & London: Harvester Wheatsheaf, 1991).

5. Simon During, "Postmodernism or Post-colonialism?" p. 369.

6. Simon During, "Postmodernism or post-colonialism today," *Textual Practice* 1:1 (Spring 1987): 33.

7. Helen Tiffin, Introduction, in *Past the Last Post*, p. xiii.

8. Helen Tiffin, "Post-Modernism, Post-Colonialism and the Rehabilitation of Post-Colonial History," p. 171.

9. A Baudrillardian term quoted in Simon During, "Postmodernism or Post-colonialism?" p. 367.

Bibliography

Primary texts

The Mystic Masseur. London: Andre Deutsch, 1957.

The Suffrage of Elvira. London: Andre Deutsch, 1958.

Miguel Street. London: Andre Deutsch, 1958.

"The Little More." *The Times*, (London), 13 July 1961, p. 13.

"Speaking of Writing." *The Times*, (London), 2 January 1964, p. 11.

"Words on Their Own." *Times Literary Supplement* (London), 4 June 1964, p. 472.

"East Indian, West Indian." *Reporter*, 17 June 1965, p. 36.

"Images." *New Statesman*, 24 September 1965, pp. 452–453.

"The Writer." *New Statesman*, 18 March 1966, pp. 381–382.

An Area of Darkness. London: Penguin Books, 1968. First published by Andre Deutsch, 1964.

The Mimic Men. London: Penguin Books, 1969. First published by Andre Deutsch, 1967.

A House for Mr Biswas. London: Penguin Books, 1969. First published by Andre Deutsch, 1961.

The Middle Passage. London: Penguin Books, 1969. First published by Andre Deutsch, 1962.

A Flag on the Island. London: Penguin Books 1969. First published by Andre Deutsch, 1967.

"Power to the Caribbean People." *New York Review of Books*, 3 September 1970, pp. 32–34.

"Without a Dog's Chance." *New York Review of Books*, 18 May 1972, pp. 29–31.

"The Corpse at the Iron Gate." *New York Review of Books*, 10 August 1972, pp. 3–4, 6–8.

Mr Stone and the Knights Companion. London: Penguin Books, 1973. First published by Andre Deutsch, 1963.

The Loss of El Dorado. London: Penguin Books, 1973. First published by Andre Deutsch, 1969.

In a Free State. London: Penguin Books, 1973. First published by Andre Deutsch, 1971.

"Conrad's Darkness." *New York Review of Books*, 17 October 1974, pp. 16–21.

The Overcrowded Barracoon. London: Penguin Books, 1976. First published by Andre Deutsch, 1972.

Guerrillas. London: Penguin Books, 1976. First published by Andre Deutsch, 1975.

India: A Wounded Civilization. London: Penguin Books 1979. First published by Andre Deutsch, 1977.

A Bend in the River. London: Penguin Books, 1980. First published by Andre Deutsch, 1979.

The Return of Eva Peron with *The Killings in Trinidad*. London: Penguin Books, 1981. First published by Andre Deutsch, 1981.

Among the Believers: An Islamic Journey. London: Penguin Books, 1982. First published by Andre Deutsch, 1981.

Finding the Centre. London: Penguin Books, 1985. First published by Andre Deutsch, 1984.

The Enigma of Arrival. London: Viking, 1987.

"On Being a Writer." *New York Review of Books*, 23 April 1987, p. 7.

A Turn in the South. London: Penguin Books, 1989.

India: A Million Mutinies Now. London: Heinemann, 1990.

"Our Universal Civilization." *New York Review of Books*, 31 January 1991, pp. 22–25.

A Way in the World. New York: Alfred Knopf, 1994.

Interviews with V. S. Naipaul

Interview by David Bates. *Sunday Times Magazine* (London), 26 May 1963, p. 12.

Interview by Francis Wyndham. *Sunday Times* (London), 10 November 1968.

"The Writer as Colonial." Interview by Adrian Rowe-Evans. *Transition* 40 (1971): 56–62.

"Without a Place." Interview by Ian Hamilton. *Times Literary Supplement* (London), 30 July 1971, p. 897.

"Life on Approval." Interview by Alex Hamilton. *The Guardian*, 4 October 1971, p. 8.

"Novelist V. S. Naipaul talks about his work to Ronald Bryden." *The Listener*, 22 March 1973, 367–370.

"Meeting V. S. Naipaul." Interview by Elizabeth Hardwick. *New York Times Book Review*, 13 May 1979, p. 1.

Mukherjee, Bharati and Boyers, Robert. "A Conversation with V. S. Naipaul." *Salmagundi* 54 (1981): 4–22.

Secondary Texts

Abbott, H. Porter. "Autobiography, Autography, Fiction: Groundwork for a Taxonomy of Textual Categories." *New Literary History* 19 (Spring 1988): 599.

Adam, I. and Tiffin, H., eds. *Past the Last Post*. New York, London: Harvester Wheatsheaf, 1991.

Anderson, Linda. "Ideas of Identity and Freedom in V. S. Naipaul and Joseph Conrad." *English Studies* 59 (December 1978): 510–517.

Auster, Paul. *The New York Trilogy*. London: Faber & Faber, 1988.

Bachelard, Gaston. *The Poetics of Space*. Boston: Beacon Press, 1979.

Barthes, Roland. *Image-Music-Text*. Translated and edited by Stephen Heath. London: Fontana, 1979.

Baugh, Edward. "Towards West Indian Criticism." *Caribbean Quarterly* 14 (March-June 1968).

Begam, Richard. "Silence and Mut(e)ilation: White Writing in J. M. Coetzee's *Foe*." *South Atlantic Quarterly* 93:1 (Winter 1994): 111–129.

Belitt, Ben. "A House for Mr Naipaul." *Salmagundi* 54 (Fall 1981): 23–42.

Bhabha, Homi K. "Signs Taken for Wonders: Questions of Ambivalence and Authority Under a Tree Outside Delhi, May 1817." In *"Race,"*

Writing and Difference, pp. 163–184. Edited by Henry Louis Gates, Jr. Chicago & London: Chicago University Press, 1985.

Blodgett, Harriet. "Beyond Trinidad." *South Atlantic Quarterly* 73 (Summer 1974): 388–403.

Boxill, Anthony. "V. S. Naipaul's Starting Point." *Journal of Commonwealth Literature* 10 (August 1975): 1–9.

Boyers, Robert. "Confronting the Present." *Salmagundi* 54 (Fall 1981): 77–97.

Brooks, Peter. "The Idea of Psychoanalytic Literary Criticism." In *Discourse in Literature and Psychoanalysis*, pp. 1–18. Edited by Shlomith Rimmon-Kenan. London: Methuen, 1987.

Bruss, Elizabeth. *Autobiographical Acts: The Changing Situation of a Literary Genre*. Baltimore & London: The Johns Hopkins University Press, 1976.

Coulthard, G. R. *Race and Colour in Caribbean Literature*. Oxford: Oxford University Press, 1962.

Cudjoe, Selwyn R. *V. S. Naipaul, A Materialist Reading*. Amherst, Mass.: The University of Massachusetts Press, 1988.

De Man, Paul. *The Rhetoric of Romanticism*. New York: Columbia University Press, 1984.

Derrick, A. C. "Naipaul's Technique as a Novelist." *Journal of Commonwealth Literature*, No. 7 (July 1969): 22–23.

Derrida, Jacques. *Writing and Difference*. Translated by Alan Bass. London: Routledge & Kegan Paul, 1978.

During, Simon. "Postmodernism or Postcolonialism?" *Landfall* 39 (1985): 366–380.

———. "Postmodernism or Post-colonialism Today." *Textual Practice* 1 (1987): 32–47.

———. "Waiting for the Post: some relations between modernity, colonization, and writing." *Ariel* 20 (1989): 31–61.

Eakin, Paul John. "Malcolm X and the Limits of Autobiography." In *Autobiography: Essays Theoretical and Critical*, pp. 181–193. Edited by James Olney. Princeton: Princeton University Press, 1980.

———. *Fictions in Autobiography: Studies in the Art of Self-Invention*. Princeton: Princeton University Press, 1985.

Enright, D. J. "*In a Free State*." In *Readings in Commonwealth Literature*. Edited by William Walsh. Oxford: Clarendon Press, 1973.

Finney, Brian. *The Inner I*. London: Faber & Faber, 1985.

Fleishman, Avrom. *Figures of Autobiography: The Language of Self-Writing in Victorian and Modern England*. Berkeley: University of California Press, 1983.

Foucault, Michel. "What is an Author?" In *Textual Strategies: Perspectives in Post-Structuralist Criticism*, pp. 141–160. Translated and edited by Josue V. Harari. London: Methuen, 1979.

Freud, Sigmund. *Family Romances. The Standard Edition of the Complete Psychological Works of Sigmund Freud*, 9 (1959), pp. 237–241. Translated from the German under the general editorship of James Strachey. 24 Vols. London: The Hogarth Press, 1953–74.

———. *The Interpretation of Dreams. The Standard Edition of the Complete Psychological Works of Sigmund Freud*, 4 (1953). Translated from the German under the general editorship of James Strachey. 24 Vols. London: The Hogarth Press, 1953–74.

———. *Totem and Taboo. The Standard Edition of the Complete Psychological Works of Sigmund Freud*, 13 (1955). Translated from the German under the general editorship of James Strachey. 24 Vols. London: The Hogarth Press, 1953–74.

———. *Beyond the Pleasure Principle. The Standard Edition of the Complete Psychological Works of Sigmund Freud*, 18 (1955), pp. 7–64. Translated from the German under the general editorship of James Strachey. 24 Vols. London: The Hogarth Press, 1953–74.

———. "The Ego and the Superego." *The Standard Edition of the Complete Psychological Works of Sigmund Freud*, 19 (1961), pp. 28–39. Translated from the German under the general editorship of James Strachey. 24 Vols. London: The Hogarth Press, 1953–74.

———. "The Dissolution of the Oedipus Complex." *The Standard Edition of the Complete Psychological Works of Sigmund Freud*, 19 (1961), pp. 173–179. Translated from the German under the general editorship of James Strachey. 24 Vols. London: The Hogarth Press, 1953–74.

Garebian, Keith. "V. S. Naipaul's Negative Sense of Place." *Journal of Commonwealth Literature* 10 (August 1975): 22–35.

———. "The Grotesque Satire of *A House for Mr Biswas*." *Modern Fiction Studies* 30 (Autumn 1984): 487–496.

Goodhart, Eugene. "V. S. Naipaul's Mandarin Sensibility." *The Partisan Review* 50 (1983): 244–256.

Gordon, David J. "Character and Self in Autobiography." *The Journal of Narrative Technique* 18 (Spring 1988): 105–119.

Gunn, Janet. *Autobiography: Toward a Poetics of Experience.* Philadelphia: University of Pennsylvania Press, 1982.

Gurr, A. J. "Third World Novels: Naipaul and After." *Journal of Caribbean Literature* 7 (June 1972): 6–13.

———. "The Freedom of Exile in Naipaul and Doris Lessing." *Ariel* 13 (October 1982): 7–18.

Gusdorf, Georges. "Conditions and Limits of Autobiography." In *Autobiography: Essays Theoretical and Critical*, pp. 28–48. Edited by James Olney. Princeton: Princeton University Press, 1980.

Gussow, Mel. "Writer without Roots." *New York Times Magazine*, 26 December 1976, p. 8.

Hamner, Robert D. "Character and Setting." In *Critical Perspectives on V. S. Naipaul*, pp. 209–241. Edited by the author. London: Heinemann, 1979.

———, ed. *Critical Perspectives on V. S. Naipaul.* London: Heinemann, 1979.

Harris, Wilson. *Tradition, the Writer and Society.* London: New Beacon, 1967.

Hart, Francis. "Notes for an Anatomy of Modern Autobiography." *New Literary History* 1 (1970): 485–511.

Hemenway, Robert. "Sex and Politics in V. S. Naipaul." *Studies in the Novel* 14 (Summer 1982): 189–202.

Hughes, Peter. *V. S. Naipaul.* London: Routledge, 1988.

Hutcheon, Linda. "'Circling the Downspout of Empire': Post-Colonialism and Post-Modernism." *Ariel* 20: 4 (October 1989): 149–175.

James, Louis, ed. *The Islands in Between.* London: Oxford University Press, 1968.

JanMohamed, Abdul R. "The Economy of Manichean Allegory: The Function of Racial Difference in Colonialist Literature." In *"Race," Writing and Difference*, pp. 78–106. Edited by Henry Louis Gates, Jr. Chicago & London: The University of Chicago Press, 1985.

Jay, Paul. *Being in the Text: Self-Representation from Wordsworth to Roland Barthes.* Ithaca & London: Cornell University Press, 1984.

Lacan, Jacques. *Ecrits: A Selection.* London: Tavistock Publications, 1977.

Lamming, George. *The Pleasures of Exile.* London: Michael Joseph, 1960.

Laplanche, Jean, & J. -B. Pontalis. *The Language of Psychoanalysis.* Translated by Donald Nicholson-Smith. London: The Hogarth Press, 1985.

Lee, R. H. "The Novels of V. S. Naipaul." In *Critical Perspectives on V. S. Naipaul*, pp. 68–83. Edited by Robert D. Hamner. London: Heinemann, 1979.

Lejeune, Philippe. "The Autobiographical Contract." In *French Literary Theory Today*, pp. 192–222. Edited by Tzvetan Todorov, translated by R. Carter. Cambridge, England: Cambridge University Press, 1982.

Lemaire, Anika. *Jacques Lacan*. Translated by David Macey. London: Routledge & Kegan Paul, 1977.

Maes-Jelinek, Hena. "The Myth of El Dorado in the Caribbean Novel." *Journal of Commonwealth Literature* 6 (June 1971): 113–128.

Malraux, Andre. *Antimemoirs*. Translated by Terence Kilmartin. London: Penguin Books, 1970.

Mandel, Barrett J. "Full of Life Now." In *Autobiography: Essays Theoretical and Critical*, pp. 49–72. Edited by James Olney. Princeton: Princeton University Press, 1980.

Mannoni, O. *Prospero and Caliban*. New York: Frederick A. Praeger, 1964.

McCarthy, Mary. *Memories of a Catholic Girlhood*. New York: Harcourt, 1957.

McSweeney, Kerry. "V. S. Naipaul: Sensibility & Schemata." *Critical Quarterly* 18 (Autumn 1976): 73–79.

———. *Four Contemporary Novelists: Angus Wilson, Brian Moore, John Fowles, V. S. Naipaul*. Montreal: McGill-Queen's University Press, 1983.

Maxwell, D. E. S. "Landscape and Theme." In *Commonwealth Literature*, pp. 82–90. Edited by John Press. London: Heinemann, 1965.

Morris, Robert K. *Paradoxes of Order*. Columbia, Missouri: University of Missouri Press, 1975.

Mukherjee, Arun P. "Whose Post-Colonialism and Whose Postmodernism?" *World Literature Written in English* 30: 2 (Autumn 1990): 1–9.

Nabokov, Vladimir. *Speak Memory*. London: Penguin Books, 1969.

Nachman, Larry David. "Psychoanalysis and Social Theory: The Origin of Society and of Guilt." *Salmagundi* 52–53 (Spring-Summer 1981): 65–106.

———. "The Worlds of V. S. Naipaul." *Salmagundi* 54 (Fall 1981): 59–76.

Naipaul, Seepersad. *The Adventures of Gurudeva and Other Stories.* London: Andre Deutsch, 1976.

Nixon, Rob. *London Calling, V. S. Naipaul, Postcolonial Mandarin.* New York, Oxford: Oxford University Press, 1992.

Nunez-Harrell, Elizabeth. "Lamming and Naipaul: Some Criteria for Evaluating the Third-World Novel." *Contemporary Literature* 19 (Winter 1978): 26–47.

Olney, James. *Metaphors of Self: The Meaning of Autobiography.* Princeton: Princeton University Press, 1972.

———. "Autobiography and the Cultural Moment: A Thematic, Historical, and Bibliographical Introduction." In *Autobiography, Essays Theoretical and Critical,* pp. 3–27. Edited by the author. Princeton: Princeton University Press, 1980.

———, ed. *Autobiography, Essays Theoretical and Critical.* Princeton: Princeton University Press, 1980.

Ormerod, D. "Theme and Image in V. S. Naipaul's *A House for Mr Biswas.*" *Texas Studies in Language and Literature* 8 (1967): 589–602.

Padhi, Bibhu. "Naipaul on Naipaul and the Novel." *Modern Fiction Studies* 30 (Autumn 1984): 455–465.

Parrinder, Patrick. "V. S. Naipaul and the Uses of Literacy." *Critical Quarterly* 21 (Summer 1979): 5–13.

Parry, Benita. "Problems in Current Theories of Colonial Discourse." *Oxford Literary Review* 9/1–2 (1987): 27–58.

Pascal, Roy. *Design and Truth in Autobiography.* Cambridge, Mass.: Harvard University Press, 1960.

Pike, Burton. "Time in Autobiography." *Comparative Literature* 28 (Fall 1976): 326–342.

Press, John, ed. *Commonwealth Literature.* London: Heinemann, 1965.

Ramchand, Kenneth. "A House for Mr Biswas." *Caribbean Quarterly* 15 (March 1969): 60–72.

———. *The West Indian Novel and Its Background.* London: Faber & Faber, 1970.

———. "Concern for Criticism." *Caribbean Quarterly* 16 (June 1970): 51–60.

Rank, Otto. *The Myth of the Birth of the Hero and Other Writings.* New York: Vintage Press, 1959.

Rimmon-Kenan, Shlomith, ed. *Discourse in Literature and Psychoanalysis.* London: Methuen, 1987.

Roberts, Sheila. "Post-colonialism, or the House of Friday—J. M. Coetzee's *Foe*." *World Literature Written in English* 31:1 (Spring 1991): 87–92.

Rohler, Gordon. "The Ironic Approach." In *The Islands in Between*. Edited by Louis James. London: Oxford University Press, 1968.

———. "Character and Rebellion in *A House for Mr Biswas*." In *Critical Perspectives on V. S. Naipaul*, pp. 84–93. Edited by Robert D. Hamner. London: Heinemann, 1979.

Salmagundi 70–71 (1986). Panel Response and Discussion: "The Intellectual in the Post-Colonial World."

Saussure, Ferdinand, de. *Course in General Linguistics*. Introduction by Jonathan Culler. London: Fontana/Collins, 1974.

Schafer, Roy. *The Analytic Attitude*. New York: Basic Books, 1983.

Sederberg, Peter C. "Faulkner, Naipaul and Zola: Violence and the Novel." In *The Artist and Political Vision*, pp. 291–316. Edited by Benjamin R. Barber & Michael J. Gargas McGarth. New Brunswick (U.S.A.) & London (U.K.): Transaction Books, 1982.

Sharpe, Jenny. "Figures of Colonial Resistance." *Modern Fiction Studies* 35/1 (1989): 137–155.

Simpson, Louis. "Disorder and Escape: The Fiction of V. S. Naipaul." *The Hudson Review* 37 (Winter 1984–85): 571–577.

Skura, Meredith. *The Literary Uses of the Psychoanalytic Process*. New Haven: Yale University Press, 1980.

Sleman, Stephen. "Modernism's Last Post." *Ariel* 20: 4 (October 1989): 3–17.

———. "Post-Colonial Allegory and the Transformation of History." *Journal of Commonwealth Literature* 23/1 (1988): 157–168.

Spence, Donald. *Narrative Truth and Historical Truth: Meaning and Interpretation in Psychoanalysis*. New York: Norton, 1982.

Spengemann, William. *The Forms of Autobiography*. New Haven & London: Yale University Press, 1980.

Sprinker, Michael. "Fictions of the Self: The End of Autobiography." In *Autobiography: Essays Theoretical and Critical*, pp. 321–342. Edited by James Olney. Princeton: Princeton University Press, 1980.

Starobinski, Jean. "The Style of Autobiography." In *Autobiography: Essays Theoretical and Critical*, pp. 73–83. Edited by James Olney. Princeton: Princeton University Press, 1980.

Sturrock, John. "The New Model Autobiographer." *New Literary History* 9 (Autumn 1977): 57–63.

Synge, H. B. "V. S. Naipaul: A Spokesman for Neo-Colonialism." *Literature and Ideology* 2 (Summer 1969): 85.

Thieme, John. "V. S. Naipaul's Third World: A Not So Free State." *Journal of Commonwealth Literature* 10 (August 1975): 10–22.

———. "Ralph Singh's Journey in *The Mimic Men*." *Modern Fiction Studies* 30 (Autumn 1984): 509.

———. *The Web of Tradition*. Hertford, England: Dangaroo Press/ Hansib Publications, 1987.

Thorpe, Michael. *V. S. Naipaul*. Harlow, Essex: Longman Group Ltd., 1976.

Tiffin, Helen. "Post-Colonialism, Post-Modernism and the Rehabilitation of Post-Colonial History." *Journal of Commonwealth Literature* 23: 1 (1988): 169–181.

Todorov, Tzvetan. *French Literary Theory Today*. Cambridge: Cambridge University Press, 1982.

Walsh, William. *A Manifold Voice*. London: Chatto & Windus, 1970.

———. *Readings in Commonwealth Literature*. Oxford: Clarendon, 1973.

Warner-Lewis, Maureen. "Cultural Confrontation, Disintegration and Syncretism in 'A House for Mr Biswas'." In *Critical Perspectives on V. S. Naipaul*, pp. 94–103. Edited by Robert D. Hamner. London: Heinemann, 1979.

Weintraub, Karl J. "Autobiography and Historical Consciousness." *Critical Inquiry* 1 (1975): 821–848.

White, Landeg. *V. S. Naipaul, A Critical Introduction*. London: Macmillan, 1975.

Wirth-Nesher, Hanna. "The Curse of Marginality: Colonialism in Naipaul's *Guerrillas*." *Modern Fiction Studies* 30 (Autumn 1984): 531–545.

Wright, Elizabeth. *Psychoanalytic Criticism*. London & New York: Methuen, 1984.

Index

Note: Bold page ranges refer to main discussion of text.